the *finer* edge

Crocheted Trims, Motifs & Borders

Kristin Omdahl

INTERWEAVE.
interweave.com

dedication

I dedicate this book to my Shark Hunter. You are my inspiration to
be the best person I can be, to work hard and smart, and to always
have fun and smile. I love you with all my heart and soul.

Editor Kim Werker ❀ *Technical Editor* Karen Manthey
Art Director Liz Quan ❀ *Cover Designer* Lora Lamm ❀ *Interior Designer* Julia Boyles
Illustrator Karen Manthey ❀ *Beauty Photographer* Joe Hancock
Swatch Photographer Joe Coca ❀ *Production Designer* Katherine Jackson

 Interweave Press LLC
201 East Fourth Street
Loveland, CO 80537-5655 USA
interweave.com

Printed in China by C&C Offset

Library of Congress Cataloging-in-Publication Data
not available at time of printing.

ISBN 978-1-59668-554-3 (pbk.)
ISBN 978-1-62033-083-8 (eBook)

10 9 8 7 6 5 4 3 2 1

acknowledgments

I wish to recognize Jaime Guthals for suggesting I write this book. We were in the green room taping *Knitting Daily TV* a couple of seasons ago, and Jaime was admiring some segments I produced for the show on crochet edgings. She asked me to consider writing my next book on it. Thanks for the great idea, Jaime! Thank you to the talented photographer and stylist for bringing my excitement and enthusiasm for this book to vivid life through gorgeous photos.

Thank you to the incredibly talented team of people I collaborate with at Interweave, including Annie Bakken, Allison Korleski, Kim Werker, Karen Manthey, and Meghan Sommer.

Contents

Up, Down, and Around the Edge

Adding an edging is a great way to spruce up and decorate your crochet projects. In this collection, I created edgings in all types of construction: top-down, bottom-up, side to side, motifs, and more. In addition, I thought of unusual ways to apply the edgings beyond the traditional framing of a project. We will make fabric from edging, make 3-dimensional projects from edging, create twisted fabric, and much more.

How to Use the Dictionary

The edgings in this dictionary are organized by construction. The first section's edgings are worked side to side (or parallel to the edge of the fabric you will join it to). The next section contains edgings worked top-down from the edge of the existing fabric to the end of the edging. The third section's edgings are worked bottom-up, from the beginning of the edging to the fabric edge. In the fourth section, I've included miscellaneous edgings that don't fit precisely into these categories. Experiment by applying different edgings to swatches you've made until you find a great match, keeping in mind that most edgings require a certain multiple of stitches for their pattern repeat, and you may need to adjust your base-fabric pattern accordingly.

To mix and match the edgings within a project, again take note of the multiple of stitches required for each pattern's repeat. It's simplest to mix and match patterns with the same number of stitches in the repeat. If the required number of stitches is close but not exact, you can add or subtract to achieve the correct count in your first row of stitches (increase or decrease accordingly to ease into the correct stitch count). Generally speaking, if you are less than 10% off on the stitch count, you should be fine making minor adjustments to accommodate your desired edging patterns.

Note: If you encounter an abbreviation that's unfamiliar to you, check the Glossary (see page 140).

Ephesus Cowl, page 86

Petra Skirt, page 130

Edging Around the Corner

There are a couple of ways to turn corners in a rectangular piece when applying an edging. In any case, you need to take into account that it takes more stitches to turn a corner with the edging remaining flat than it does to work the edging in a straight line, so you almost always need to work increases at the corner and/or on either side of it.

The most straightforward way to add fullness in a pattern involving a stitch repeat is to increase for a full additional repeat on either side of the corner on the first row or round of the edging. For example, let's say your edging-stitch repeat is 5 stitches. I would work a round of single or double crochet and increase at the corners to accommodate an additional repeat on either side. You can do this one of two different ways:

Work 3 stitches each in the 2 stitches on either side of the center corner stitch and in the center corner stitch for a total of 15 stitches (increasing by 2 full pattern repeats).

Or, for the 5 stitches before and 5 stitches after the corner, work 2 stitches in each stitch for a total of 20 stitches (4 repeats of the 5-stitch repeat of the edging on the subsequent rows/rounds).

Once this set-up row is established, you are ready to work the edging rows or rounds in pattern without needing to alter for corner fullness.

Alternatively, you can insert an extra repeat little bits at a time at the corners to eventually create a full extra repeat of the stitch pattern. This works well if the edging consists of multiple rows or rounds, but I suggest sketching the edging chart to figure out how to gradually add stitches to replicate the growth of an additional stitch pattern repeat.

One final approach is to increase in simple stitches at the corner rather than in the pattern stitch, but it will stand out as a wedge against the rest of the edging pattern; that said, it could add a welcome decorative touch.

If you are making the edging separate from the fabric to apply later, you could even gather or pleat the edging to create the fullness required for turning the corner. In the case of the Luxor Blanket (see page 102), we change direction on the stand-alone edging—by 90 or 270 degrees—to create the corners to wrap around the completed afghan.

Luxor Blanket, page 102

Top-Down *Edgings*

Birch Scallops

✿ Multiple of 30 + 1 sts.
✿ Swatch: (30 × 3) + 1 = 91 sts.

Ch 92 for swatch as shown.

Row 1: Sc in 2nd ch from hook and each ch across, turn—91 sc.

Rows 2–3: Ch 1, sc in each st across.

Edging
Row 1 (RS): Ch 1, sc in first sc, *[ch 4, sk 4 sts, sc in next st] 2 times, ch 1, sk next 4 sts, (tr, ch 1) 7 times in next st, sk next 4 sts, sc in next st, [ch 4, sk 4 sts, sc in next st] 2 times; rep from * across, turn.

Row 2: Ch 1, sc in first sc, *ch 4, sk next ch-4 sp, sc in next sc, ch 2, [tr in next tr, ch 2] 7 times, sk next ch-4 sp, sc in next sc, ch 4, sc in next sc; rep from * across, turn.

Row 3: Ch 1, (sc, ch-3 picot, sc) in first sc, * [ch 3, ch-3 picot, 3-tr cl in next tr) 7 times, ch 3, sk next ch-4 sp, (sc, ch-3 picot, sc) in next sc; rep from * across, turn.

Fasten off.

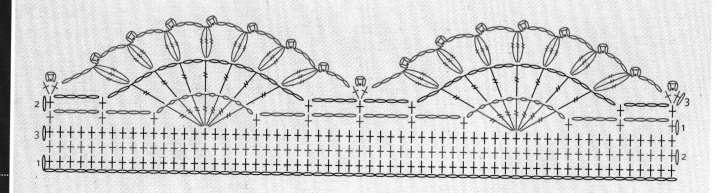

Textured Waves

- ❀ Multiple of 9 sts, grows into multiple of 17 sts.
- ❀ Swatch: (9 × 5) = 45 sts; grows to (17 × 5) = 85 sts

Ch 46 for swatch as shown.

Row 1: Sc in 2nd ch from hook and in each ch across, turn—45 sts.

Rows 2-3: Ch 1, sc in each st across, turn.

Edging

Row 1 (WS): Ch 3 (counts as dc), 4 dc in first st, dc in each of next 7 sts, 5 dc in next st, *5 dc in next st, dc in each of next 7 sts, 5 dc in next st; rep from * across, turn—85 sts.

Row 2: Ch 1, fpsc in each st across, turn.

Row 3: Ch 3 (counts as dc), working in front of fpsc row, in tops of sts 2 rows below, 4 dc in first st, (sk next st, dc in next st) 7 times, 5 dc in next st, *5 dc in next st, (sk next st, dc in next st) 7 times, 5 dc in next st; rep from * across, turn.

Row 4: Rep Row 2.

Rows 5-8: Rep Rows 3-4 twice.

Fasten off.

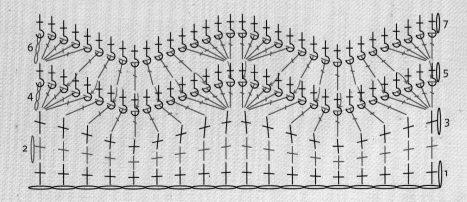

Mermaid Scales

☼ Multiple of 8 + 1 sts.
☼ Swatch: (8 × 5) + 1 = 41 sts.

Ch 42 for swatch as shown.

Row 1 (RS): Sc in 2nd ch from hook and in each ch across, turn—41 sc.

Row 2: Ch 1, sc in first st, ch 1, sk 1 st, sc in next st, *ch 5, sk 3 sts, sc in next st**, ch 3, sk 3 sts, sc in next st; rep from * across, ending last rep at **, ch 1, sk 1 st, sc in last st.

Row 3: Ch 1, sc in first st, *11 dc in next ch-5 sp**, working over ch-3 sp, sc in center st 2 rows below; rep from * across, ending last rep at **, sc in last st, turn.

Row 4: Ch 6 (counts as tr, ch 2), sk 3 dc, sc in next dc, ch 3, sk 3 dc, sc in next dc, *ch 5, sk 7 sts, sc in next dc, ch 3, sk 3 dc, sc in next dc; rep from * across to last 4 sts, ch 2, sk 3 sts, tr in last sc, turn.

Row 5: Ch 3, 5 dc in first ch-2 sp, *working over ch-3 sp, sc in center st 2 rows below**, 11 dc in next ch-5 sp; rep from * across, ending last rep at **, sc in st below next ch-3 sp, 6 dc in last ch-2 sp, turn.

Row 6: Ch 1, sc in first st, ch 1, sk 1 st, sc in next st, *ch 5, sk 7 sts, sc in next dc, ch 3, sk 3 dc, sc in next dc; rep from * across, ending last rep at **, ch 1, sk 1 dc, sc in last dc, turn.

Rows 7–10: Rep Rows 3–6.

Rows 11–12: Rep Rows 3–4.

Row 13: Rep Row 5.

Row 14: Sl st in first st, *ch 1, sk 1 st, sl st in next st; rep from * across.

Fasten off.

Reduced Sample of Pattern

✿ **tip**

This is an interesting edging because it can be used as a beautiful allover fabric or as a bold geometric edging, depending on how long you want to repeat. The nature of its offset pattern allows it to easily be decreased at a 45-degree angle.

Multi-level Orchid

✿ Multiple of 7 ch-5 sps + 3 ch-5 sps.
✿ Swatch: (7 × 3) + 3 = 24 ch-5 sps.

Set-up Row: (Ch 4, tr in 4th ch from hook) 24 times for swatch as shown.

Row 1 (RS): Ch 4 (counts as dc, ch 1 here and throughout), sc in first ch-4 sp on side edge of Set-up Row, (ch 5, sc) in each ch-4 sp across, ch 1, dc in ch at base of last tr, turn—23 ch-5 sps.

Row 2: Ch 1, sc in first ch-1 sp, (ch 5, sc) in each ch-5 sp across, ending with last sc in 3rd ch of beg ch-4, turn—24 ch-5 sps.

Row 3: Ch 4, sc in first ch-5 sp, (ch 5, sc) in each ch-5 sp across, ch 1, dc in last sc, turn.

Rows 4–7: Rep Rows 2–3 twice.

Row 8: Ch 1, sc in first ch-1 sp, (ch 5, sc) in next 4 ch-5 sps, *ch 3, (dc, ch 8, dc) in next ch-5 sp, ch 3, sc in next ch-5 sp**, (ch 5, sc) in each of next 5 ch-5 sps; rep from * across, ending last rep at **, (ch 5, sc) in each of next 3 ch-5 sps, ch 5, sc in 3rd ch of beg ch-4, turn.

Row 9: Ch 4, sc in first ch-5 sp, (ch 5, sc) in each of next 3 ch-5 sps, *ch 3, sk next ch-3 sp, sl st in next ch-8 sp, (ch 3, 2 dc, ch-3 picot, 2 dc, ch 3, sl st) 3 times in same sp, ch 3, sc in next ch-5 sp**, (ch 5, sc) in next 4 ch-5 sps; rep from * across, ending last rep at **, (ch 5, sc) in next 3 ch-5 sps, ch 1, dc in last sc, turn.

Row 10: Ch 1, sc in first ch-1 sp, *(ch 5, sc) in next 3 ch-5 sps**, ch 3, [(dc, ch 8, dc) in next picot, ch 5] twice, (dc, ch 8, dc) in next picot, ch 3, sc in next ch-5 sp; rep from * across, ending last rep at **, sc in 3rd ch of beg ch-4, turn.

Row 11: Ch 4, sc in first ch-5 sp, (ch 5, sc) in next 2 ch-5 sps, *ch 2, sk next ch-3 sp, [(sl st, ch 3, 2 dc, ch-3 picot, 2 dc, ch 3, sl st) 3 times in next ch-8 sp, ch 4] twice, (sl st, ch 3, 2 dc, ch-3 picot, 2 dc, ch 3, sl st) 3 times in next ch-8 sp, ch 2, sc in next ch-5 sp, (ch 5, sc) in next 2 ch-5 sps; rep from * across, ending with ch 1, dc in last sc.

Fasten off.

10

8

6

4

2

Set-up Row

11

9

7

5

3

1

Reduced Sample of Pattern

✿ tip

***This is one of the more elaborate
edgings*** in the collection. I think it would be
fitting for the edging on a silk shawl worn while
tango dancing or visiting royalty at a formal
ball. It's not necessarily difficult to make, but its
ornamented, bold shape makes it oh so dramatic.

Three Rows of Teeth

✿ Multiple of 4 + 1 sts.

✿ Swatch: (9 × 4) + 1 = 37 sts.

Ch 38 for swatch as shown.

Row 1: Sc in 2nd ch from hook and in each ch across, turn—37 sc.

Rows 2–3: Ch 1, sc in each sc across, turn.

Edging

Row 1 (RS): Ch 1, (sc, ch 3, 4 dc) in first st, *sk 3 sts, (sc, ch 3, 4 dc) in next st; rep from * across to last 4 sts, sk 3 sts, sc in last st, turn.

Row 2: Ch 5, sk next 3 dc, sc in next ch-3 sp, *ch 3, sk next 3 dc, sc in next ch-3 sp; rep from * across.

Row 3: Ch 1, (sc, ch 3, 4 dc) in first st, *sk next ch-3 sp, (sc, ch 3, 4 dc) in next sc; rep from * across to last ch-3 sp, sk next 3 ch, sc in next ch, turn.

Row 4: Rep Row 2.

Row 5: Ch 1, (sc, ch 3, ch-3 picot, 4 dc) in first st, *sk next ch-3 sp, (sc, ch 3, ch-3 picot, 4 dc) in next sc; rep from * across to last ch-3 sp, sk next 3 ch, sc in next ch.

Fasten off.

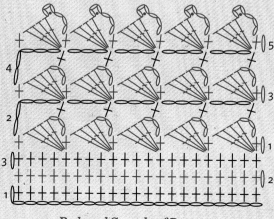

Reduced Sample of Pattern

Tiered Offset Shells in Rows

❋ Multiple of 8 + 2 sts.

❋ Swatch: (8 × 6) + 2 = 50 sts.

Ch 51 for swatch as shown.

Row 1: Sc in 2nd ch from hook and in each ch across, turn—50 sc.

Rows 2-3: Ch 1, sc in each sc across, turn.

Edging

Row 1 (WS): Ch 1, sc in first st, ch 2, *sc in each of next 3 sts, (sc, ch 6, sl st) in next st, sc in each of next 4 sts, ch 2; rep from * across, sc in last st, turn.

Row 2: Ch 2, *sc in next ch-2 sp, (5 dc, ch-3 picot, 5 dc) in next ch-6 sp; rep from * across, sc in last ch-2 sp, turn.

Row 3: Ch 1, (sc, ch 6, sl st) in first sc, *ch 3, working behind sts in last row, sk next 3 sc 2 rows below, (sc, ch 2, sl st) in next sc, ch 3**, (sc, ch 6, sl st) in next ch-2 sp 2 rows below; rep from * across, ending last rep at **, (sc, ch 3, dc) in last sc in current row (counts as ch-6 sp), turn.

Row 4: Ch 3 (counts as dc), ch-3 picot, 5 dc in ch-3 sp, *sk next ch-3 sp, sc in next ch-2 sp**, sk next ch-3 sp, (5 dc, ch-3 picot, 5 dc) in next ch-6 sp; rep from * across, ending last rep at **, (5 dc, ch-3 picot, ch 3, sl st) in last ch-6 sp, turn.

Row 5: Ch 1, (sc, ch 2, sl st) in sc 2 rows below, *ch 3, working behind sts in last row, sk next 3 sc 2 rows below, (sc, ch 6, sl st) in ch-2 sp, sk next ch-3 sp, (sc, ch 2, sl st) in next sc; rep from * across, turn.

Row 6: Rep Row 2.

Fasten off.

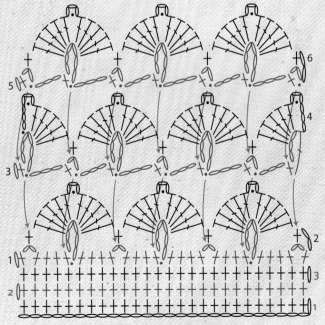

Reduced Sample of Pattern

Herringbone Texture

❀ Multiple of 3 + 2 sts.
❀ Swatch: (3 × 11) + 2 = 35 sts.

Ch 36 for swatch as shown.

Row 1: Sc in 2nd ch from hook and in each ch across, turn—35 sc.

Rows 2–3: Ch 1, sc in each sc across, turn.

Edging

Row 1 (WS): Ch 3 (counts as dc), sk first dc, *sk 1 st, dc in each of next 2 sts, dc in last skipped st; rep from * across, dc in last st, turn.

Rows 2–6: Rep Row 1.

Row 7: Ch 1, working from left to right, reverse sc in each st across, turn.

Fasten off.

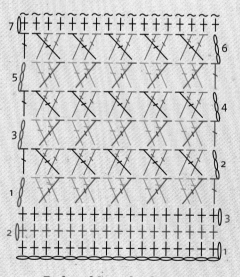

Reduced Sample of Pattern

Sl St Textured

✿ Multiple of any number of sts.

✿ Ch any number of sts.

Row 1: Sc in 2nd ch from hook and in each ch across, turn.

Rows 2-3: Ch 1, sc in each sc across, turn.

Edging
Row 1 (WS): Ch 1, sl st in flp of first sc, (ch 1, sl st) in flp of each st across, turn.

Row 2: Working in free lps of sts 2 rows below, ch 1, sc in blp of each st across, turn.

Rep Rows 1–2 for patt.

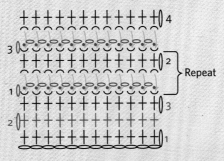

Reduced Sample of Pattern

 tip

> ***This dense, non-curling edging*** is simple to learn and invaluable for a variety of purposes. Try swapping out your favorite ribbing on a hat; making a bold, thick frame for a rug; or putting warm cuffs on a coat's sleeves.

Circle Coins

* Multiple of 8 + 1 sts.
* Swatch: (8 × 8) + 1 = 65 sts.

Ch 66 for swatch as shown.

Row 1: Sc in 2nd ch from hook and each ch across, turn—65 sc.

Rows 2-6: Ch 1, sc in each st across, turn.

Edging

Row 1: Ch 1, sc in first st, *ch 5, sk 3 sts, sc in next st; rep from * across, turn.

Row 2: Ch 1, *5 sc in next ch-5 sp, ch 10, sl st in side of last sc worked, work 4 more sc in same ch-5 sp, 5 sc in next ch-5 sp, turn, 9 sc in top of last ch-10 lp, turn, 9 sc in bottom of ch-10 lp, sl st in side of last sc worked in ch-5 sp, 4 more sc in same ch-5 sp; rep from * across.

Fasten off.

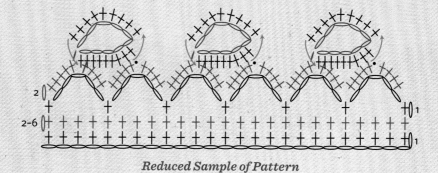

Reduced Sample of Pattern

Cresting Waves

✿ Multiple of 12 + 1 sts.

✿ Swatch: (12 × 5) + 1 = 61 sts.

Ch 62 for swatch as shown.

Row 1: Sc in 2nd ch from hook and in each ch across, turn—61 sts.

Rows 2–6: Ch 1, sc in each st across, turn.

Edging

Row 1: Ch 1, sc in first st, *[ch 5, sk 3 sts, sc in next st] twice, ch 2, sk 3 sts, dc in next st (counts as ch-5 sp), turn, ch 5, sc in next ch-5 sp, ch 2, dc in next ch-5 sp (counts as ch-5 sp), turn, ch 1, tr in next ch-5 sp (counts as ch-5 sp), turn, ch 3, 6-dc in next ch-5 sp, 5 dc in each of next 2 ch-5 sps, sl st in next sc in prev row; rep from * across, turn.

Fasten off.

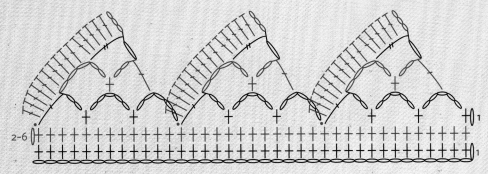

Reduced Sample of Pattern

Superior Flower
(as featured in Persepolis Top, page 112)

✿ Multiple of 8 + 5 sts.
✿ Swatch: (8 × 6) + 5 = 53 sts.

Ch 54 for swatch as shown.

Row 1: Sc in 2nd ch from hook and in each ch across, turn—53 sc.

Rows 2-6: Ch 1, sc in each st across, turn.

Edging

Row 1 (WS): Ch 1, sc in first st, *ch 5, sk 3 sts, sc in next st; rep from * across, turn—13 ch-5 sps.

Row 2: Sl st in next ch-5 sp, ch 6 (counts as tr, ch 2), (tr, [ch 2, tr] 4 times) in same sp, *(sc, ch 5, sc) in next ch-5 sp, turn, (ch 5, sc) 3 times in ch-5 sp, turn, (sl st, ch 3, 2 dc, ch-4 picot, 2 dc, ch 3, sl st) in each of next 3 ch-5 sps, (tr, [ch 2, tr] 5 times) in next ch-5 sp in Row 1; rep from * across.

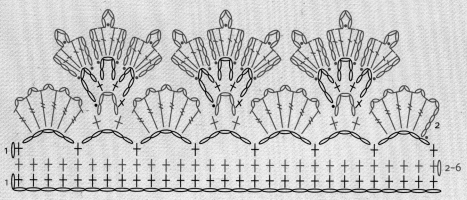

Reduced Sample of Pattern

Spade

- ✿ Multiple of 6 + 1 sts.
- ✿ Swatch: (6 × 10) + 1 = 61 sts.

Ch 62 for swatch as shown.

Row 1: Sc in 2nd ch from hook and in each ch across, turn—61 sc.

Rows 2–6: Ch 1, sc in each st across, turn.

Edging

Row 1 (WS): Ch 4, tr in same st (counts as 2-tr cl), ch 4, 2-tr cl in same st, *sk 5 sts, (2-tr cl, ch 4, 2-tr cl) in next st; rep from * across, turn.

Row 2: Ch 1, sc in first st, *(sl st, ch 3, 3-dc cl, ch-3 picot, ch 3, sl st) in next ch-4 sp**, sc2tog over next 2 sts; rep from * across, ending last rep at **, sc in last st.

Fasten off.

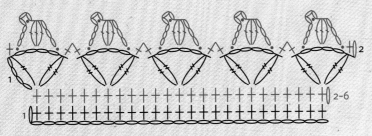

Reduced Sample of Pattern

Open Leaf

✿ Each section is a multiple of 20 + 10 for beg chain.

Row 1: Ch 10, sc in 2nd ch from hook and in each of next 8 ch, *ch 20, sc in 2nd ch from hook and in each of next 8 ch; rep from * for desired width, turn.

Row 2: Sl st in each of last 9 sts on prev row, ch 7 (counts as trtr, ch 1), *working in back side of 9 ch, [trtr in next ch, ch 1] twice, [trtr in next ch, ch 2] 3 times, dtr in next ch, ch 2, tr in next ch, ch 2, dc in next ch, ch 2, sc in next ch, working in beg ch,

sc in each of next 10 ch, over next 9 sc work: sc in next sc, ch 2, dc in next sc, ch 2, tr in next sc, ch 2, dtr in next sc, ch 1, turn, sk next 8 ch-2 sps, sl st in next ch-2 sp on prev petal, ch 1, turn, trtr in next ch, [ch 2, trtr in next sc] twice, [ch 1, trtr in next sc] twice**, ch 3; rep from * across, ending last rep at **, ch 1, trtr in end ch.

Fasten off.

Pin leaf-tip points, spray block.

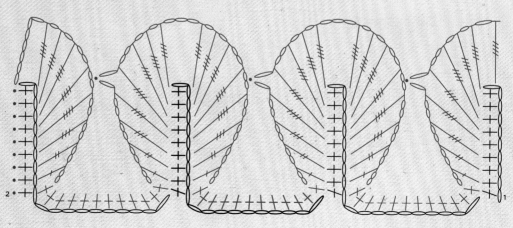

Reduced Sample of Pattern

Closed Leaf *(as featured in Palmira Shawl, page 120)*

✿ Each section is a multiple of 20 + 10 for beg chain

Row 1: Ch 10, sc in 2nd ch from hook and in each of next 8 ch, *ch 20, sc in 2nd ch from hook and in each of next 8 ch; rep from * for desired width, turn.

Row 2: Ch 1, *over next 8 sts on prev row, sc in next 2 sc, hdc in next 2 sc, dc in next 2 sc, tr in next 2 sc, 4 tr in next sc, ch-4 picot, working in back side of chains, 4 tr in next ch, tr in next 2 ch, dc in next 2 ch, hdc in next 2 ch, sc in next 2 ch**, working in beg ch, sc in each of next 10 ch; rep from * across, ending last rep at **, turn.

Row 3: Sl st in next 12 sts, sl st in next picot, ch 1, sc in same picot, *ch 7, sk 2 sts, yo twice, insert hook in next st, (yo, pull through 2 lps twice), sk 2 sts, yo 3 times, insert hook in next st, (yo, pull through 2 lps) 3 times, sk next 6 sts on this leaf, 10 sc on base ch, and next 6 sts on next leaf, yo 3 times, insert hook in next st, (yo, pull through 2 lps) 3 times, sk next 2 sts, yo twice, insert hook in next st, (yo, pull through 2 lps twice), yo, pull through all 5 lps on hook (2tr/2dtr cl worked), ch 7, sc in next ch-4 picot; rep from * across.

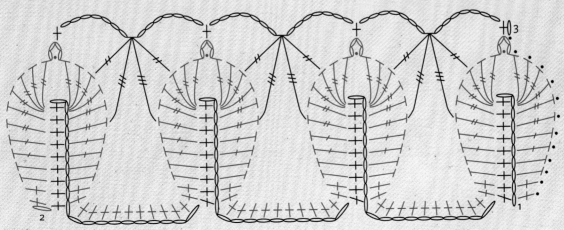

Reduced Sample of Pattern

Gothic Cathedral
(as featured in Palmira Shawl, page 120)

❀ Multiple of 18 + 1 sts.
❀ Swatch: (18 × 5) + 1 = 91.

Ch 92 for swatch as shown.

Row 1: Sc in 2nd ch from hook and in each ch across, turn—91 sc.

Rows 2–3: Ch 1, sc in each st across, turn.

Edging

Row 1: Ch 1, sc in first 4 sts, ch 5, sk 4 sts, dc2tog over next 2 sts, *ch 5, sk 4 sts, sc in each of next 3 sts, turn, [ch 2, dc] 3 times in next ch-5 sp, ch 2, (dc, ch 5, dc) in next dc2tog, [ch 2, dc] 3 times in next ch-5 sp, sk next 2 sc, sl st in next sc, turn, [ch 2, dc in next dc] 4 times, ch 2, (dc, ch 5, dc) in next ch-5 sp, [ch 2, dc in next dc] 4 times, sc in each of next 5 sc in prev row, *ch 5, sk 4 sts, dc2tog over next 2 sts, ch 5, sk 4 sts, sc in each of next 3 sts, turn, [ch 2, dc] 3 times in next ch-5 sp, ch 2, (dc, ch 5, dc) in next dc2tog, [ch 2, dc] 3 times in next ch-5 sp, sk next 2 sc, sl st in next sc, turn, [ch 2, dc in next dc] 3 times, ch 9, turn, sk next 5 ch-2 sps, sl st in next dc, turn, ([3 sc, ch-3 picot] 3 times, 3 sc) in next ch-9 lp, sl st in next dc, ch 2, dc in next dc, ch 2, (dc, ch 5, dc) in next ch-5 sp, [ch 2, dc in next dc] 4 times**, sc in each of next 5 sc in prev row; rep from * across, ending last rep at **, sc in last sc.

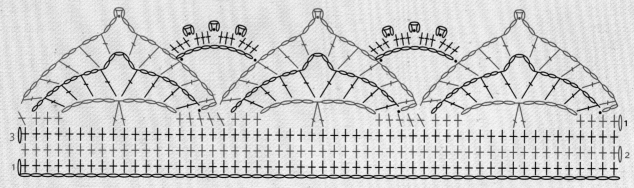

Reduced Sample of Pattern

Foundation Petal

- Multiple of 6 + 3 sts.
- Swatch: (11 × 6) + 3 = 69 sts.

Ch 70 for swatch as shown.

Row 1: Sc in 2nd ch from hook and each ch across—69 sts.

Rows 2–6: Ch 1, sc in each st across.

Edging

Row 1: Ch 3 (counts as dc), dc in each of next 2 sts, *ch 3, etr in 3rd ch from hook, edtr in base of last st, etr in base of last st, ch 3, sk 3 sts in prev row, dc in each of next 3 sts; rep from * across. Fasten off.

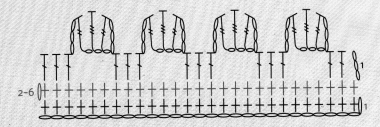

Reduced Sample of Pattern

Oval Small Pearl

- ✿ Multiple of 3 + 1 sts.
- ✿ Swatch: (3 × 22) + 1 = 67 sts.

Ch 68 for swatch as shown.

Row 1: Sc in 2nd ch from hook and in each ch across—67 sc.

Rows 2–8: Ch 1, sc in each st across.

Edging

Row 1: Ch 1, sc in first st, *ch 3, 2-dc cl in side of last sc worked, sk 2 sts, sc in next st; rep from * across. Fasten off.

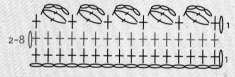

Reduced Sample of Pattern

 tip

This delicate edging adds a dainty touch to projects from baby items to home decor. The small pearls add a softness to an otherwise flat-edged fabric.

Oval Large Pearl (3 strings of pearls)

✿ Multiple of 5 + 1 sts.

✿ Swatch: (5 × 13) + 1 = 66 sts.

Ch 67 for swatch as shown.

Row 1: Sc in 2nd ch from hook and in each ch across, turn—66 sc.

Rows 2–8: Ch 1, sc in each st across, turn.

Edging

Row 1: Ch 1, sc in first st, *ch 5, 3-dtr cl in side of last sc worked, sk 4 sts, sc in next st; rep from * across, turn.

Row 2: Ch 8 (counts as dc, ch 5), dc in next sc, *ch 5, dc in next sc; rep from * across.

Row 3: Ch 1, sc in first st, *ch 5, 2-dtr cl in side of last st worked, sc in next dc; rep from * across.

→ **Note:** *The row of chains in Row 2 sits next to the underside of the 2-dtr cl and looks like an extra leg. So, the first row of pearls needs to be compensated by working 3-dtr cl.*

Row 4: Rep Row 2.

Row 5: Rep Row 3. Fasten off.

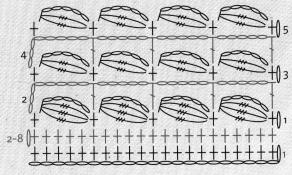

Reduced Sample of Pattern

Deco Scallops

☸ Multiple of 13 sts.
☸ Swatch: (13 × 5) = 65 sts.

Ch 66 for swatch as shown.

Row 1: Sc in 2nd ch from hook and in each ch across—65 sts in swatch.

Rows 2–6: Ch 1, sc in each st across.

Edging

→ **Note:** *Scallop begins by slip-stitching in the center of the scallop, then working back and forth on a section and gaining more of the scallop at the end of each turn.*

Row 1: *Sl st in each of the first 4 sts, sk 2 sts, 15 dc in next st, sk 2 sts, sl st in next st, ch 3, sk 2 sts, sl st in next st, turn, [ch 3, sk 2 dc, dc in next dc] 5 times, sk 2 sts on prev row, sl st in next st, turn, (sc, ch 3, sc, ch 3, sc) in next 5 ch-3 sps, sl st in next sc on prev row; rep from * across.

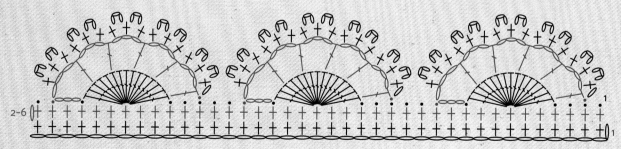

Reduced Sample of Pattern

Deco Fan & Scallops

❀ Multiple of 26 + 1 sts.

❀ Swatch: (26 × 3) + 1 = 79 sts.

Ch 80 for swatch as shown.

Row 1: Sc in 2nd ch from hook and in each ch across—79 sts.

Rows 2–6: Ch 1, sc in each st across.

Edging

→ *Note: Scallop begins by slip-stitching in the center of the scallop, then working back and forth on a section and gaining more of the scallop at the end of each turn.*

Row 1: Ch 5 (counts as dtr), 6 dtr in first st, sk 3 sts, **sl st in each of next 8 sts, ch 5, sk 3 sts, sl st in next sc, ch 3, sk next sc, sl st in next sc, turn, 12 dc in next ch-5 sp, sk 2 sts in prev row, sl st in next st, ch 3, sk 2 sts, sl st in next st, turn, [ch 2, sk 1 dc, dc in next dc] 6 times, ch 2, sk next dc, sk next sc in prev row, sl st in next sc, ch 3, sk next sc, sl st in next st, turn, 3 dc in each of next 7 ch-3 sps, sk next sc in prev row, sl st in next sc, turn, [ch 5, sk next dc, sl st in next dc] 10 times, ch 5, sk next 2 dc, sl st in next sc in prev row, sk next 3 sc, 13 dtr in next st, sk next 3 sts; rep from * across to last 4 sts, sk next 3 sts, 7 dtr in last st. Fasten off.

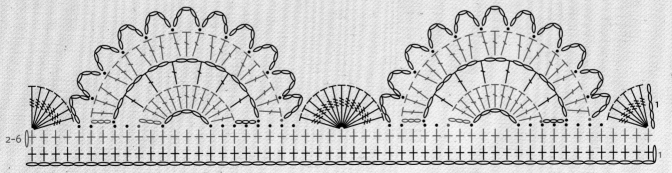

Reduced Sample of Pattern

Bottom-Up *Edgings*

Belled Scallops

☼ Multiple of 22 + 4 sts.

☼ Swatch: (22 × 5) + 4 = 114 sts.

Ch 115 for swatch as shown.

Row 1: Hdc in 2nd ch from hook and in each ch across, turn—114 hdc.

Row 2: Ch 1, sc in each of first 4 hdc, ch 4, sk 2 sts, (tr5tog, picking up a leg every 3rd st), ch 4, sk 2 sts, sc in each of next 5 sts, *ch 4, sk 2 sts, (tr5tog, picking up a leg every 3rd st), ch 4, sk 2 sts; rep from * across to last 4 sts, sc in each of last 4 sts, turn.

→ **Note:** *Edging complete, now begin regular pattern, except multiple is now 12 + 3 (as shown: (12 × 5) + 3 = 63 sts). The following rows constitute a sample main project pattern.*

Row 3: Ch 1, sc in first 4 hdc, *3 sc in next ch-4 sp, sc in next cl, 3 sc in next ch-4 sp, sc in next 5 sc; rep from * across, ending last rep at **, sc in last 4 sts.

Row 4: Ch 1, sc in each sc across, turn.

Rep Row 4 for desired length.

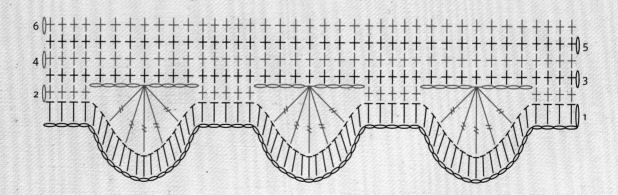

Rolled/Twisted

✿ Multiple of 5 + 2 sts.
✿ Swatch: (5 × 6) + 2 = 32.

Ch 33 for swatch as shown.

Row 1: Hdc in 2nd ch from hook and in each ch across, turn—32 hdc.

Row 2: Ch 1 (does not count as a st), hdc in each hdc across, turn.

Row 3: Ch 1, hdc in first hdc, twist top edge toward back and bottom edge toward top, working in foundation ch, hdc in each of next 5 ch, *twist top edge toward back and bottom edge toward top, sk 5 hdc in Row 2, hdc in next 5 hdc, twist top edge toward back and bottom edge toward top, sk 5 ch of foundation ch, hdc in each of next 5 ch; rep from * across to last st, twist top edge toward back and bottom edge toward top, hdc in last st, turn.

→ **Note:** *Edging complete, now begin regular pattern. Multiple to remain the same. The following rows constitute a sample main project pattern.*

Row 4: Ch 1, hdc in each hdc across, turn.

Rep Row 4 for desired length.

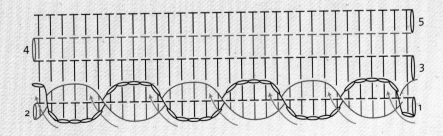

Picot Straight

✿ Multiple of 2 + 2 sts.

Row 1: Ch 2, fsc in 2nd ch from hook, *ch-3 picot, work 2 fsc; rep from * across.

Row 2: Working on ch side of foundation sts, ch 1, sc in each st across bottom edge of Row 1, turn.

Row 3: Ch 1, sc in each sc across, turn.

Rep Row 3 for desired length.

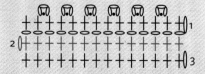

❀ *tip*

Simple and elegant, this edging is perfect for any bottom-up project, and the use of foundation stitches gives the edge a more relaxed feel than a chain beginning. If you are making something that requires blocking, the evenly spaced picots help in pinning for a perfect, finished shape.

Picot Scalloped

✿ Multiple of 10 sts.

Row 1: Ch 2, fsc in 2nd ch from hook, *ch-3 picot, work 2 fsc; rep from * across. (Swatch shown repeats from * 30 times—60 fsc.)

Row 2: Working on ch side of foundation sts, ch 1, *sc in each of next 2 foundation sts on bottom edge of Row 1, [insert hook in next st, yo and pull up a lp, sk next 4 sts, insert hook in next st, yo and pull up a lp, yo and pull through all lps on hook—sc2tog worked over 6 sts], sc in each of next 2 foundation sts; rep from * across—30 sts in swatch.

Row 3: Ch 1, sc in each st across—30 sc in swatch.

Rep Row 3 for desired length.

❋ *tip*

Try practicing your foundation stitches

on this beautifully textured edge. It would be especially lovely on a skirt hem or the lower "V" of a triangular shawl worked from the bottom up. Make sure to take into account how much the width decreases from the original foundation stitches to the scalloped edging when designing with this one.

Reduced Sample of Pattern

Two-color Egg

❋ Multiple of 5 + 1 sts.

Row 1: With color A, *ch 5, dtr in 5th ch from hook; rep from * 10 more times, drop yarn, leaving lp long so it won't ravel.

Row 2: Join color B with sl st in ch-5 sp at beg of Row 1, ch 3 (counts as dc), work (3 dc, ch 1, 3 dc) in each ch-5 sp across, dc in last st, turn.

Row 3: Ch 3, work (3 dc, ch 1, 3 dc) in each ch-1 sp across, dc in last st. Fasten off.

Row 4: Pick up lp of color A from end of Row 1, ch 6, sl st in top of ch-3 at beg of Row 3, ch 5 (counts as dc, ch 2), sc in next ch-1 sp, ch 2, *working under both rows of color B, dtr in sp between 2 shells 2 rows below, ch 2, sc in next ch-1 sp, ch 2; rep from * across, trtr in first ch of beg ch in Row 1.

Row 5: Ch 1, sc in same st, *ch 4, sk next 2 ch-2 sps, sc in next dtr; rep from * across, ending with last sc in 3rd ch of beg ch-5, turn.

Row 6: Ch 3 (counts as dc), *4 dc in next ch-4 sp, dc in next st; rep from * across, turn.

Row 7: Ch 3 (counts as dc), dc in each st across, turn.

Rep Row 7 for desired length. Fasten off.

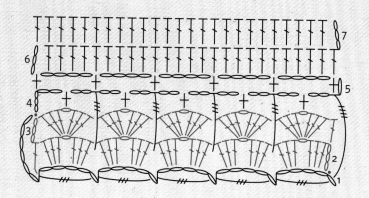

Faux Embellished 4-petal Flowers I

✿ Multiple of 12 + 4 sts.

✿ Swatch: (12 × 5) + 4 = 64.

Ch 66 for swatch as shown.

Row 1: Dc in 4th ch from hook (beg ch-3 counts as dc), dc in each of next 2 ch, *[ch 2, sk 2 ch, dc in next ch] 3 times, dc in next 3 ch; rep from * across, turn.

Row 2: Ch 3 (counts as dc), dc in each of next 3 sts, *(ch 2, dc in next dc) twice, turn 90 degrees counterclockwise and working along side of post of dc just worked, (sl st, ch 3, 3 dc, ch 3, sl st) around post of dc, turn 90 degrees counterclockwise and working in ch-2 sp on prev row, work (sl st, ch 3, 3 dc, ch 3, sl st) in ch-2 sp, turn 90 degrees counterclockwise and working in side of post of next dc, work (sl st, ch 3, 3 dc, ch 3, sl st) around post of dc, turn work 90 degrees counterclockwise and working in ch-2 sp on current row, work (sl st, ch 3, 3 dc, ch 3, sl st) in ch-2 sp, ch 2, sk next ch-2 sp, dc in each of next 4 sts; rep from * across, turn.

Row 3: Ch 3 (counts as dc), dc in each of next 3 sts, *[ch 2, sk next ch-2 sp, dc in next dc] 3 times, dc in each of next 3 dc; rep from * across, turn.

Row 4: Ch 1, sc in each of first 4 sts, *[2 sc in ch-2 sp, sc in next dc] 3 times, sc in each of next 3 sts; rep from * across, turn.

Row 5: Ch 1, sc in each st across, turn.

Rep Row 5 for desired length.

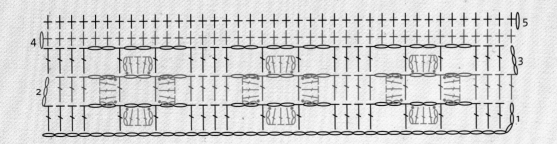

Faux Embellished 4-petal Flowers II, Offset

✿ Multiple of 12 + 4 sts.
✿ Swatch: (12 × 5) + 4 = 64.

Ch 66 for swatch as shown.

Row 1: Dc in 4th ch from hook (beg ch-3 counts as dc), dc in each of next 2 ch, *[ch 2, sk 2 ch, dc in next ch] 3 times, dc in next 3 ch; rep from * across, turn.

Row 2: Ch 3 (counts as dc), dc in each of next 3 sts, *(ch 2, dc in next dc) twice, turn 90 degrees counterclockwise and working along side of post of dc just worked, work (sl st, ch 3, 3 dc, ch 3, sl st) around post of dc, turn 90 degrees counterclockwise and working in ch-2 sp on prev row, work (sl st, ch 3, 3 dc, ch 3, sl st) in ch-2 sp, turn 90 degrees counterclockwise and working in side of post of next dc, work (sl st, ch 3, 3 dc, ch 3, sl st) around post of dc, turn work 90 degrees counterclockwise and working in ch-2 sp on current row, work (sl st, ch 3, 3 dc, ch 3, sl st) in ch-2 sp, ch 2, sk next ch-2 sp, dc in each of next 4 sts; rep from * across, turn.

Row 3: Ch 3 (counts as dc), dc in each of next 3 dc, *[ch 2, sk next ch-2 sp, dc in next dc] 3 times, dc in each of next 3 dc; rep from * across, turn.

Row 4: Ch 3 (counts as dc), dc in next 3 dc, *[2 dc in next ch-2 sp, dc in next dc] 3 times, dc in next 3 dc; rep from * across, turn.

Row 5: Ch 5 (counts as dc, ch 2), sk first 3 dc, dc in next dc, ch 2, skip 2 sts, dc in next 4 dc, *[ch 2, sk 2 sts, dc in next dc] 3 times, dc in next 3 dc; rep from * across, ending with [ch 2, sk 2 sts, dc in next dc] twice, turn.

Row 6: Ch 5 (counts as dc, ch 2), sk first ch-2 sp, dc in next dc, ch 2, sk 2 sts, dc in next 4 dc, *(ch 2, dc in next dc) twice, turn 90 degrees counterclockwise and working along side of post just worked, work (sl st, ch 3, 3 dc, ch 3, sl st) around post of dc, turn 90 degrees counterclockwise and working in ch-2 sp on prev row, work (sl st, ch 3, 3 dc, ch 3, sl st) in ch-2 sp, turn 90 degrees counterclockwise and working in side of post of next dc, work (sl st, ch 3, 3 dc, ch 3, sl st) around post of dc, turn work 90 degrees counterclockwise and working in ch-2 sp on current row, work (sl st, ch 3, 3 dc, ch 3, sl st) in ch-2 sp, ch 2, sk next ch-2 sp, dc in each of next 4 sts; rep from * across, ending with [ch 2, sk 2 sts, dc in next dc] twice, turn.

Row 7: Ch 5 (counts as dc, ch 2), sk first ch-2 sp, dc in next dc, ch 2, sk 2 sts, dc in next 4 dc, *[ch 2, sk next ch-2 sp, dc in next dc] 3 times, dc in each of next 3 dc; rep from * across, ending with [ch 2, sk 2 sts, dc in next dc] twice, turn.

Row 8: Ch 3 (counts as dc), [2 dc in next ch-2 sp, dc in next dc] twice, dc in next 3 dc, *[2 dc in next ch-2 sp, dc in next dc] 3 times, dc in next 3 dc; rep from * across, ending with [2 dc in next ch-2 sp, dc in next dc] twice, turn.

Row 9: Ch 3 (counts as dc), dc in each of next 3 dc, *[ch 2, sk next 2 sts, dc in next dc] 3 times, dc in each of next 3 dc; rep from * across, turn.

Rows 10–11: Rep Rows 2–3.

Row 12: Ch 1, sc in first 4 dc, *[2 sc in next ch-2 sp, sc in next dc] 3 times, sc in next 3 dc; rep from * across, turn.

Row 13: Ch 1, sc in each sc across, turn.

Rep Row 13 for desired length.

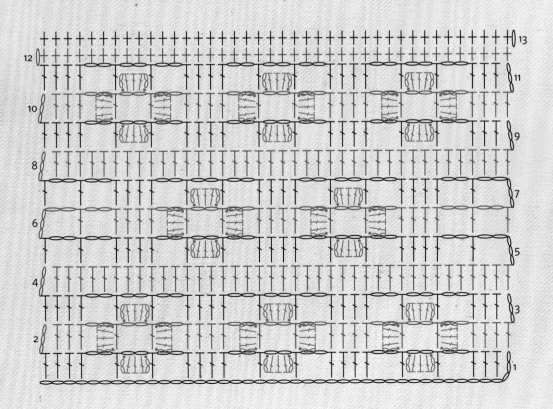

Faux Embellished 4-petal Flowers III

✿ Multiple of 9 + 1 sts.

✿ Swatch: (9 × 6) + 1 = 46.

Ch 50 for swatch as shown.

Row 1: Dc in 9th ch from hook (first 5 ch count as dc, ch 2), *ch 2, sk 2 ch, dc in next ch; rep from * across, turn—18 ch-2 sps.

Row 2: Ch 5 (counts as dc, ch 2), sk first ch-2 sp, dc in next dc, *ch 2, sk next ch-2 sp, dc in next dc, turn 90 degrees counterclockwise and working along side of post of dc just worked, work (sl st, ch 3, 3 dc, ch 3, sl st) around post of dc, turn 90 degrees counterclockwise and working in ch-2 sp on prev row, work (sl st, ch 3, 3 dc, ch 3, sl st) in ch-2 sp, turn 90 degrees counterclockwise and

working in side of post of next dc, work (sl st, ch 3, 3 dc, ch 3, sl st) around post of dc, turn work 90 degrees counterclockwise and working in ch-2 sp on current row, work (sl st, ch 3, 3 dc, ch 3, sl st) in ch-2 sp, ch 2, sk next ch-2 sp, dc in next dc; rep from * across, turn.

Row 3: Ch 5 (counts as dc, ch 2), sk first ch-2 sp, dc in next dc, *ch 2, sk next ch-2 sp, dc in next dc; rep from * across, turn.

Row 4: Ch 1, sc in first dc, *2 sc in next ch-2 sp, sc in next dc; rep from * across, turn.

Row 5: Ch 1, sc in each sc across, turn.

Rep Row 5 for desired length.

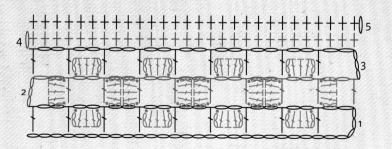

Ephesus Cowl, page 86

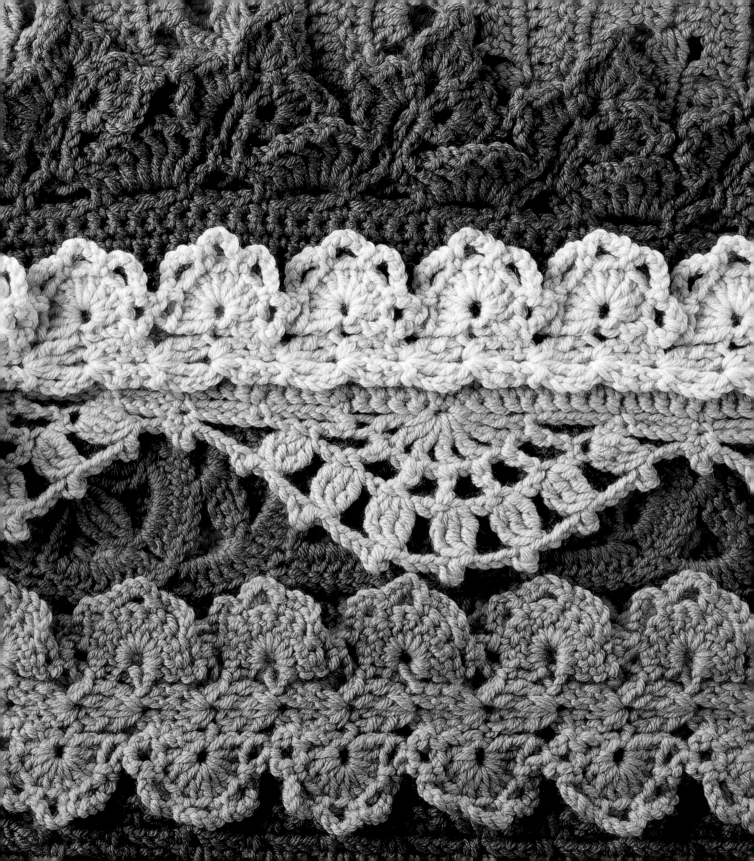

Side-to-Side
Edgings

Pinecone

Ch 14.

Row 1: 3 dc in 4th ch from hook, ch 4, sk 4 ch, sc in next ch, ch 4, sk 4 ch, 4 dc in next ch, turn.

Row 2: Sl st in next 3 sts, ch 3 (counts as dc here and throughout), 3 dc in same st, ch 5, sk next ch-5 sp, sc in next sc, ch 5, sk next ch-5 sp, 4 dc in next dc, turn, leaving rem sts unworked.

Row 3: Sl st in next 3 sts, ch 3, 3 dc in same st, ch 6, sk next ch-5 sp, sc in next sc, ch 6, sk next ch-5 sp, 4 dc in next dc, turn, leaving rem sts unworked.

Row 4: Sl st in next 3 sts, ch 3, 3 dc in same st, sk next 2 ch-6 sps, 4 dc in next dc, turn, leaving rem sts unworked.

Rows 5-6: Ch 3, 3 dc in same st, sk next 6 sts, 4 dc in next dc, turn.

Row 7: Ch 3, 3 dc in same st, ch 4, sk 3 sts, sc in sp before next st, ch 4, sk next 3 sts, 4 dc in last dc, turn.

Rep Rows 2–7 for desired length, ending with Row 6 of pattern. Fasten off.

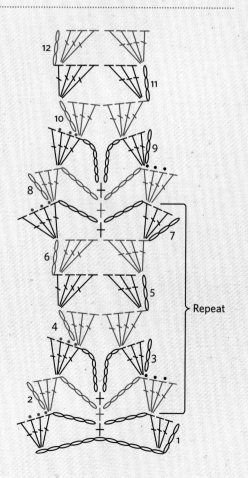

Graduated Shells in Bruges Lace

(as featured in Babylonia Hat, page 134)

Ch 9.

Row 1: 2 dc in 8th ch from hook, ch 2, 2 dc in last ch, turn.

Row 2: Ch 7, (3 dc, ch 2, 3 dc) in next ch-2 sp, turn.

Row 3: Ch 7, (4 dc, ch 2, 4 dc) in next ch-2 sp, turn.

Row 4: Ch 7, (3 dc, ch 2, 3 dc) in next ch-2 sp, turn.

Row 5: Ch 7, (2 dc, ch 2, 2 dc) in next ch-2 sp, turn.

Row 6: Ch 7, (dc, ch 2, dc) in next ch-2 sp, turn.

Row 7: Ch 7, (2 dc, ch 2, 2 dc) in next ch-2 sp, turn.

Rep Rows 2–7 for pattern. Fasten off.

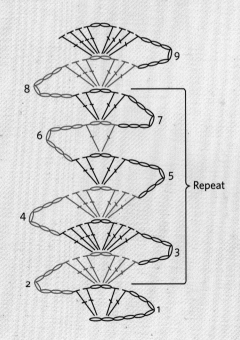

Open Medallion

Ch 7.

Row 1: 2 tr in 5th ch from hook, ch 2, tr in next ch, ch 2, 3 tr in last ch, turn.

Row 2: Ch 4 (counts as tr here and throughout), tr2tog over next 2 sts, ch 5, sk next ch-2 sp, dc in tr, ch 5, sk next ch-2 sp, tr3tog over last 3 sts, turn.

Row 3: Ch 4, 2 tr in same st, ch 2, sk next ch-5 sp, dc in dc, ch 2, sk next ch-5 sp, 3 tr in last st, turn.

Row 4: Ch 4, tr2tog over next 2 sts, sk next ch-2 sp, tr in next dc, sk next ch-2 sp, tr3tog over last 3 sts, turn.

Row 5: Ch 4, 2 tr in same st, ch 2, tr in next tr, ch 2, 3 tr in last st, turn.

Rep Rows 2–5 for pattern, ending with Row 5. Fasten off.

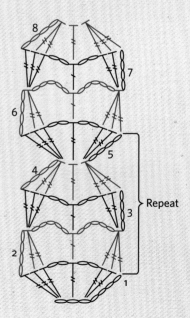

Tr Shell with 3-petal Flower on Sides

(as featured in Ephesus Cowl, page 86)

Ch 4.

Row 1: (3 tr, ch 2, 4 tr) in 4th ch from hook, ch 5, sl st in 5th ch from hook to form ring.

Row 2: (Ch 3, dc, ch 3, sl st) 3 times in ch-5 sp, ch 3, sk next 4 tr, sl st in next ch-2 sp.

Row 3: Ch 4 (counts as tr), (3 tr, ch 3, 4 tr) in same ch-2 sp, ch 5, sl st in 5th ch from hook to form ring.

Rep Rows 2–3 for pattern, ending with Row 2. Fasten off.

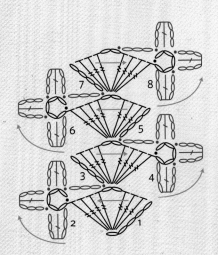

Double-sided Flower Ribbon

Row 1: Ch 4, 3 tr in 4th ch from hook, ch 5, sl st in 5th ch from hook to form ring.

Row 2: Ch 3, 10 dc in ch-5 ring, turn, ch 5, sk first 2 sts, sc in next st, [ch 5, sk 1 st, sc in next st] 4 times.

Row 3: Sk 2 tr in prev row, 4 tr in sp before next st, ch 5, sl st in 5th ch from hook to form ring.

Row 4: Rep Row 2.

Row 5: Sk 2 tr in prev row, 4 tr in sp before next st, ch 5, sl st in 5th ch from hook to form ring.

Row 6: Ch 3, 10 dc in ch-5 ring, turn, ch 2, sl st in top ch-5 sp on adjacent flower, ch 2, sk first 2 sts, sc in next st, [ch 5, sk 1 st, sc in next st] 4 times.

Rep Rows 5–6 for pattern, ending with Row 5.

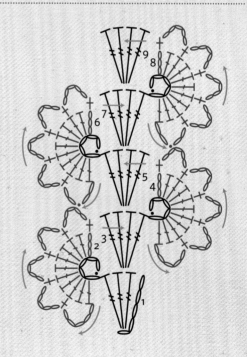

Single-sided Flower Ribbon

Ch 4.

Row 1: 3 tr in 4th ch from hook, ch 5, sl st in 5th ch from hook to form ring.

Row 2: Ch 3, 10 dc in ch-5 ring, turn, ch 5, sk 2 sts, sc in next st, [ch 5, sk 1 st, sc in next st] 4 times.

Row 3: Sk 2 tr in prev row, 4 tr in sp before next st, turn.

Row 4: Sl st in sp between 2nd and 3rd tr, ch 4 (counts as tr), work 3 tr in same sp, ch 5, sl st in 5th ch from hook to form ring.

Row 5: Ch 3, 10 dc in ch-5 ring, turn, ch 2, sl st in top ch-5 sp on adjacent flower, ch 2, sk first 2 sts, sc in next st, [ch 5, sk 1 st, sc in next st] 4 times.

Rep Rows 3–5 for pattern, ending with Row 3. Fasten off.

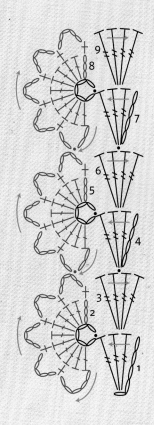

Flower Cut-Out Strips
(as featured in Pompeii Möbius, page 90)

Ch 18.

Row 1: Dc in 6th ch from hook and each ch across, turn—13 dc.

Row 2: Ch 5 (does not count as a st), dc in first 5 dc, ch 3, sk next st, 3-dc cl in next st, ch 3, sk next st, dc in each of next 5 sts, turn.

Row 3: Ch 5 (does not count as a st), dc in first 2 dc, ch 3, 2-dc cl in side of last st worked, sk 3 sts, sc in next ch-3 sp, sc in next st, sc in next ch-3 sp, ch 3, 2-dc cl in side of last st worked, sk 3 dc, dc in each of next 2 sts, turn.

Row 4: Ch 5 (does not count as a st), dc in first 2 dc, ch 7, sk next ch-3 sp, sc in next 3 sc, ch 7, sk next ch-3 sp, dc in each of last 2 dc, turn.

Row 5: Ch 5 (does not count as a st), dc in first 2 dc, 3 dc in next ch-7 sp, sk next sc, ch 3, 3-dc cl in next sc, ch 3, sk next sc, 3 dc in next ch-7 sp, dc in each of last 2 dc, turn.

Row 6: Ch 5 (does not count as a st), dc in first 5 dc, dc in next ch-3 sp, dc in next st, dc in next ch-3 sp, dc in next 5 dc, turn.

Row 7: Ch 5, dc in each dc across, turn.

Rep Rows 2–7 for pattern, ending with Row 7. Fasten off.

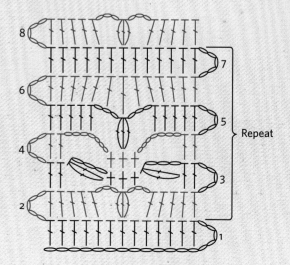

Faux Ribbed Scallops

Ch 6.

Row 1: Hdc in 3rd ch from hook (ch-2 does not count as a st), hdc in each ch across, turn—5 hdc.

Row 2: Ch 1, hdc-tbl in each st across to last st, 3 hdc-tbl in last st, turn—7 hdc.

Row 3: Ch 1, 3 hdc-tbl in first st, hdc-tbl in each st across, turn—9 hdc.

Rows 4-5: Rep Rows 2-3—13 sts after Row 5.

Row 6: Ch 1, hdc-tbl in each st across to last 3 sts, hdc3tog-tbl over last 3 sts, turn—11 sts.

Row 7: Ch 1, hdc3tog-tbl over first 3 sts, hdc-tbl in each st across—9 sts.

Rows 8-9: Rep Rows 6-7—5 hdc after Row 9.

Rep Rows 2-9 for desired length, ending with Row 9 of pattern.

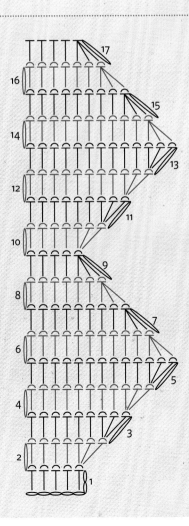

Mesh Triangle Scallops

Ch 4.

Row 1: 5 tr in 4th ch from hook, turn.

Row 2: Sl st in sp between 3rd and 4th sts, ch 4 (counts as tr here and throughout), work 5 tr in same sp, ch 2, sk 2 sts, dc in next st, turn.

Row 3: Ch 5 (counts as dc, ch 2), sk next ch-2 sp, dc in next dc, ch 2, sk next 2 sts, 6 tr in sp before next st, turn.

Row 4: Sl st in sp between 3rd and 4th sts, ch 4, work 5 tr in same sp, ch 2, sk 2 sts, dc in next dc, [ch 2, sk next ch-2 sps, dc in next st] twice, turn.

Row 5: Ch 5 (counts as dc, ch 2), sk next ch-2 sp, dc in next st, [ch 2, sk next ch-2 sp, dc in next st] twice, ch 2, sk 2 sts, 6 tr in sp before next st, turn.

Row 6: Sl st in sp between 3rd and 4th sts, ch 4, work 5 tr in same sp, ch 2, sk 2 sts, dc in next st, [ch 2, sk next ch-2 sps, dc in next st] 4 times, turn.

Row 7: Ch 5 (counts as dc, ch 2), sk next ch-2 sp, dc in next st, [ch 2, sk next ch-2 sp, dc in next st] 4 times, ch 2, sk 2 sts, 6 tr in sp before next st, turn.

Rep Rows 2–7 for pattern.

Final Row: Turn to work across zigzag edge, sl st in sp between 3rd and 4th sts, sl st in each of next 3 sts, sl st in first ch-2 sp, (ch 3, sc) twice in same ch-2 sp, *(sc, ch 3, sc, ch 3, sc) in each ch-2 sp across to corner sp, ([sc, ch 3] 4 times, sc) in corner ch-5 sp, (sc, ch 3, sc, ch 3, sc) in each row-end st to valley; rep from * across. Fasten off.

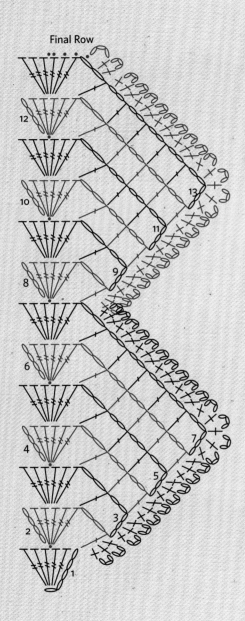

Final Row

✿ tip

This edging is crocheted sideways, which means you could either make it first, before your main project, or join it as you go to an in-progress project. You could even make it all by itself for a long, skinny wrap-around-your-neck-twice trendy accessory.

Lace Column Scallops

❀ Multiple of 6 + 3 sts.

❀ Swatch: (6 × 5) + 3 = 33 sts.

Ch 34 for edging as shown.

Row 1: Sc in 2nd ch from hook and each ch across, turn—33 sc.

Row 2: Ch 4, tr in same st (counts as tr2tog), *ch 1, sk 1 st, tr2tog in next st; rep from * across, turn.

Row 3: Ch 1, sc in same st, *sc in next ch-1 sp, sc in next st; rep from * across, turn.

Row 4: Ch 3 (counts as dc here and throughout), sk first st, dc in each of next 2 sts, *ch 3, sk 3 sts, dc in each of next 3 sts; rep from * across, turn.

Row 5: Ch 6 (counts as dc, ch 3 here and throughout), sk first 3 sts, 3 dc in next ch-3 sp, *ch 3, sk 3 dc, 3 dc in next ch-3 sp; rep from * across, ending with ch 3, sk 2 sts, dc in top of ch-3, turn.

Row 6: Ch 3, 2 dc in ch-3 sp, *ch 3, sk 3 sts, 3 dc in next ch-3 sp; rep from * across, (ch 2, tr) 6 times in next row-end st, sk next row, sl st in end of next sc row, turn, [sl st, ch 3, 2-dc cl, ch 3, sl st] in next 6 ch-2 sps.

Row 7: *Sc in next 3 dc**, 3 sc in next ch-3 sp; rep from * across, ending last rep at **, turn.

Rep Rows 2–7 for pattern, ending with Row 7.

✲ tip

Adjust the number of stitches in the pattern to make any width fabric. This would make a pretty afghan, shawl, or scarf all on its own. Use it for sleeves and the flowers turn into a frilly, feminine cuff.

Lace Column Scallops II
(as featured in Petra Skirt, page 130)

❀ Multiple of 6 + 3 sts.

❀ Swatch: (6 × 5) + 3 = 33 sts.

With color A, ch 34 for edging as shown.

Row 1: Sc in 2nd ch from hook and each ch across, turn—33 sc.

Row 2: Ch 4, tr in same st (counts as tr2tog), *ch 1, sk 1 st, tr2tog in next st; rep from * across, turn.

Row 3: Ch 1, sc in same st, *sc in next ch-1 sp, sc in next st; rep from * across, turn.

Row 4: Ch 3 (counts as dc here and throughout), sk first st, dc in each of next 2 sts, *ch 3, sk 3 sts, dc in each of next 3 sts; rep from * across, turn.

Row 5: Ch 6 (counts as dc, ch 3 here and throughout), sk first 3 sts, 3 dc in next ch-3 sp, *ch 3, sk 3 dc, 3 dc in next ch-3 sp; rep from * across, ending with ch 3, sk 2 sts, dc in top of ch-3, turn.

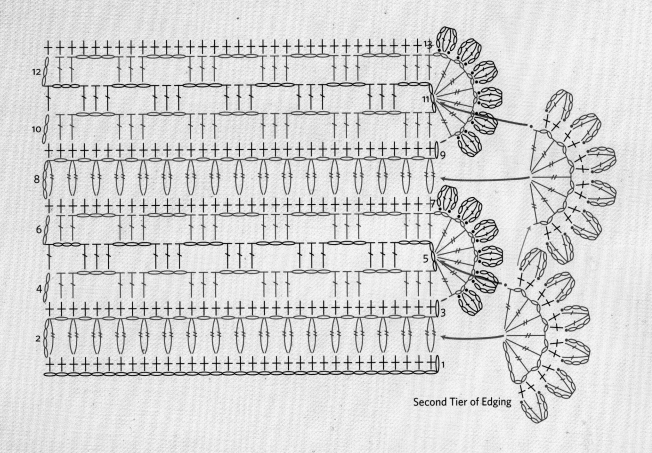

Second Tier of Edging

Row 6: Ch 3, 2 dc in ch-3 sp, *ch 3, sk 3 sts, 3 dc in next ch-3 sp; rep from * across, (ch 2, tr) 6 times in in next row-end st, sk next row, sl st in end of next sc row, turn, [sl st, ch 3, 2-dc cl, ch 3, sl st] in next 6 ch-2 sps.

Row 7: *Sc in next 3 dc**, 3 sc in next ch-3 sp; rep from * across, ending last rep at **, turn.

Rep Rows 2–7 for pattern, ending with Row 7.

Second tier of edging:

With RS facing, join color B with sl st in side of last tr at end of Row 2 on scallop side of edging.

Row 1: Ch 6 (counts as tr, ch 2), work [(tr, ch 2) 5 times, tr] in same row-end st, working behind scallops, sk next 2 row-end sts, sl st in next row-end st at base of prev scallop, turn, 2 sc in next 6 ch-2 sps, turn, [sl st in next st, ch 3, dc2tog over next same st and next st, ch 3, sl st in same st] 6 times, *sk next 2 row-end sts, [(tr, ch 2) 6 times, tr] in next row-end tr, working behind scallops, sk next 2 row-end sts, sl st in next row-end st at base of prev scallop, turn, 2 sc in next 6 ch-2 sps, turn, [sl st in next st, ch 3, dc2tog over next same st and next st, ch 3, sl st in same st] 6 times; rep from * across.

Reversible Interlocking Vertical Stripes *(as featured in Birka Car Coat, page 94)*

❀ Multiple of 8 + 4 sts.
❀ Swatch: (8 × 3) + 1 = 25 sts.

With color A, ch 28 for edging as shown.

Row 1: 2 dc in 4th ch from hook, ch 3, sk next 7 ch, *(2 dc, ch 1, 2 dc) in next ch, ch 3, sk 7 ch; rep from * across to last ch, 3 dc in last ch, drop color A to be picked up later, do not turn.

Row 2: With RS facing, join color B with sl st in top of ch-3 at beg of last row, *ch 3, working over ch-3 sp, sk next 3 ch sts in foundation ch 2 rows below, (2 dc, ch 1, 2 dc) in next ch; rep from * across, ending with ch 1, hdc in top of last dc, turn.

Row 3: Pick up color A, ch 3 (counts as dc), 2 dc in same st, *ch 3, working over ch-3 sp in last row, (2 dc, ch 1, 2 dc) in same color ch-1 sp 2 rows below; rep from * across, ending with ch 3, 3 dc in top of ch-3 two rows below, drop color A to be picked up later, do not turn.

Row 4: Pick up color B, ch 3 (working the first ch around the color B ch-3 to bring yarn to front), *working over ch-3 sp in last row, (2 dc, ch 1, 2 dc) in same color ch-1 sp 2 rows below, ch 3; rep from * across, ending with ch 1, hdc in top of last dc, turn.

Rep Rows 3–4 for pattern.

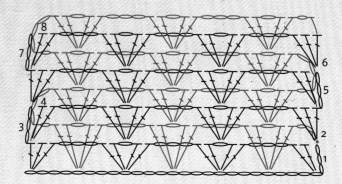

Clustered Mini-web

Ch 12.

Row 1: 4-dc cl in 4th ch from hook, ch 7, sk next 7 ch, 5-dc cl in last ch, turn.

Row 2: Ch 3, 4-dc cl in first st (counts as 5-dc cl), ch 3, sc under next 2 ch-7 sps, dc5tog in next st, turn.

Row 3: Ch 3, 4-dc cl in first st (counts as 5-dc cl), ch 7, sk next 2 ch-3 sps, 5-dc cl in last st, turn.

Rows 4-5: Ch 3, 4-dc cl in first st (counts as 5-dc cl), ch 7, sk next ch-7 sp, 5-dc cl in next st, turn.

Row 6: Ch 3, 4-dc cl in first st (counts as 5-dc cl), ch 3, sc under next 3 ch-7 sps, dc5tog in next st, turn.

Rep Rows 3–6 for pattern.

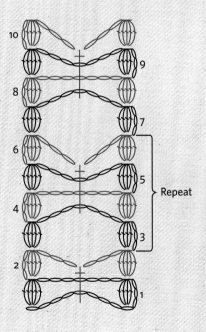

Flower-fringed Web
(as featured in Palmira Shawl, page 120)

Ch 16.

Row 1: Dc in 4th ch from hook, ch 11, sk next 11 ch, 2 dc in last ch, turn.

Row 2: Sl st in sp between first 2 dc, ch 3 (counts as dc here and throughout), dc in same sp, ch 5, sc under next 2 ch-11 lps, ch 5, sk next dc, 2 dc in sp before last dc, turn.

Row 3: Sl st in sp between 2 dc, ch 3 (counts as dc), dc in same sp, ch 11, sk next ch-11 lp, sk next dc, 2 dc in sp before last dc, turn.

Row 4: Ch 8, sl st in 6th ch from hook to form a ring, ch 2, sk next dc, 2 dc in sp before next dc, ch 11, sk next ch-11 sp, sk next dc, 2 dc in sp before last dc, turn.

Row 5: Sl st in sp between first 2 dc, ch 3, dc in same sp, ch 5, sc under next 2 ch-11 lps, ch 5, sk next dc, 2 dc in sp before last dc, (2-dc cl, [ch 2, 2-dc cl] 5 times) in next ch-6 ring, sk next row-end st, sl st in next row-end st, turn, (sl st, ch 3, 2-dc cl, ch 3, sl st) in next 5 ch-2 sps, turn.

Rows 6–7: Rep Row 3.

Rep Rows 2–7 for pattern, ending with Row 5.

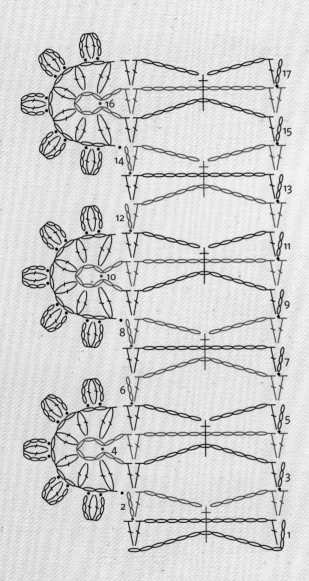

✿tip

Adjust the web section (chains) for a wider or narrower strip, or add multiples of the web to create a wider fabric still.

Miscellaneous *Edgings*

Woven Ribbon

❉ Mesh Background: Multiple of 4 + 1 sts.
❉ Swatch: (4 × 17) + 1 = 69 sts.

Mesh Background

Ch 74.

Row 1: Dc in 10th ch from hook (first 9 ch count as ch 3, dc, ch 3), *ch 3, sk 3 ch, dc in next ch; rep from * across, turn—17 ch-3 sps.

Rows 2–6: Ch 6 (counts as dc, ch 3), sk next ch-3 sp, dc in next dc, *ch 3, sk next ch-3 sp, dc in next dc; rep from * across, ending with last dc in 3rd ch of turning ch, turn.

Fasten off.

Ribbon

(make 1 for each row of mesh background)

Row 1: Ch 4 (counts as tr), 3 tr in 4th ch from hook, turn.

Row 2: Sl st in sp between 2nd and 3rd sts, ch 4 (counts as tr), 3 tr in same sp.

Rep Row 2 until piece measures desired length to weave through the spaces for the width of the mesh background. Fasten off.

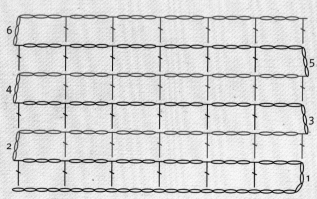

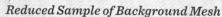

Reduced Sample of Background Mesh

Ribbon

2-Color Woven Ribbon

Worked the same as 1-color (see previous page), except using 1 color for grid and 1 color for the ribbons.

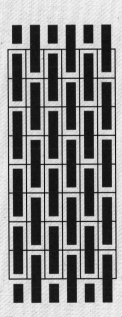

Weaving Pattern Across Rows

 tip

The volume of these interwoven strips is so dense and warm! This would make a wonderful cowl, scarf, or decorative throw-pillow covers. Use it as embellishment on a coat or sweater as cuffs, hem, collars, or front bands.

3-Color Braided Woven Ribbon

Worked the same as for 1-color (see page 68), except using 1 color for mesh background and making 3 colors for separate ribbons that are braided (per illustration) within the grid.

Weaving Pattern Across Rows

Faux Overlapping Mini-wheel Motifs
(as featured in Anni Belt/Scarf, page 108)

Motif 1

Ch 4, sl st in 4th ch from hook to form ring.

Rnd 1 (RS): Ch 4 (counts as dc, ch 1), [dc, ch 1] 7 times in ring, sl st in 3rd ch of beg ch-4 to join, turn.

Rnd 2: Sl st in next ch-1 sp, ch 3 (counts as dc), 3 dc in same ch-1 sp, 4 dc in each ch-1 sp around, sl st in top of beg ch-3 to join.

Motif 2

Row 1: Ch 4, sk 2 sts on last rnd of prev motif, sl st in each of next 3 sts, turn, ([dc, ch 1] 5 times, dc) in next ch-4 sp, sk next 2 sts on last rnd of prev motif, sl st in each of next 3 sts, turn.

Row 2: 4 dc in each ch-1 sp across, sk next st on last rnd of prev motif, sl st in next st, turn.

Motif 3

Row 1: Sl st in each of next 9 sts on last rnd of prev motif, ch 4, sk next 2 sts, sl st in each of next 3 sts, turn, ([dc, ch 1] 5 times, dc) in next ch-4 sp, sk next 2 sts on last rnd of prev motif, sl st in each of next 3 sts, turn.

Row 2: 4 dc in each ch-1 sp across, sk next st on last rnd of prev motif, sl st in next st.

Rep Motif 3 for desired length.

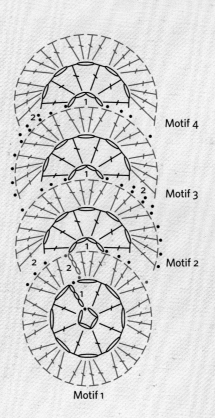

Motif 4

Motif 3

Motif 2

Motif 1

Faux Overlapping Circle Motifs
(as featured in Luxor Blanket, page 102)

Motif 1

→ **Note:** *The first motif is worked in rnds, but all subsequent motifs are worked in rows. To maintain consistency, turn work after each rnd of first motif so fabric alternates RS and WS as in all rem motifs.*

Ch 4, sl st in 4th ch from hook to form ring.

Rnd 1 (RS): Ch 3 (counts as dc here and throughout), 11 dc in ring, sl st in top of beg ch-3 to join, turn—12 dc.

Rnd 2: Ch 3, dc in first st, 2 dc in each st around, sl st in top of beg ch-3 to join, turn—24 dc.

Rnd 3: Ch 3, dc in first st, dc in next st, *2 dc in next st, dc in next st; rep from * around, sl st in top of beg ch-3 to join, turn—36 dc.

Rnd 4: Ch 3, dc in first st, dc in next 2 sts, *2 dc in next st, dc in next 2 sts; rep from * around, sl st in top of beg ch-3 to join, do not turn—48 dc.

Motif 2

Row 1: Ch 4, sk next 2 sts, sl st in each of next 3 sts on last rnd of last motif, turn, 9 dc in ch-4 sp, sk 1 st on last rnd of last motif, sl st in each of next 3 sts, turn.

Row 2: 2 dc in each st across, sk 1 st on last rnd of last motif, sl st in each of next 3 sts, turn.

Row 3: *2 dc in next st, dc in next st; rep from * across, sk 1 st on last rnd of last motif, sl st in each of next 3 sts, turn.

Row 4: *2 dc in next st, dc in each of next 2 sts; rep from * across, sk 1 st on last rnd of last motif, sl st in next st, turn.

Motif 3

Sl st in each of next 17 sts.

Rep Rows 2–4 of Motif 2.

Rep Motif 3 for desired length.

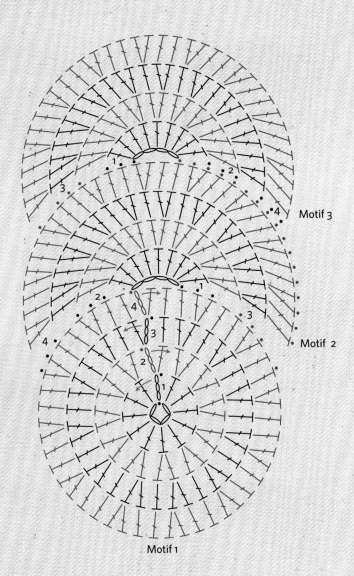

Motif 3

Motif 2

Motif 1

✿tip

I love this edging and would make miles of it if I had the time. I think the look of overlapping motifs without the sewing is so fascinating. It is incredibly easy to crochet and can be used to embellish so many kinds of projects, such as afghans, scarves, or anything that would benefit from a bold statement. You could also make one strip into a scarf or a belt or make several strips and join them together to create an interesting fabric of overlapping motifs.

Faux Overlapping Flower-in-band Motif

Motif 1

Ch 6, sl st in 6th ch from hook to form ring.

Rnd 1 (RS): Ch 5 (counts as dtr), 2-dtr cl in ring, (ch 4, 3-dtr cl) 5 times in ring, ch 4, sl st in top of first cl to join, turn—6 ch-4 sps.

Rnd 2: Sl st in next ch-4 sp, ch 3 (counts as dc), 7 dc in same sp, 8 dc in each ch-4 sp around, sl st in top of beg ch-3 to join, turn—48 dc.

Motif 2

Row 1: Sl st in next 3 sts on last rnd of prev motif, ch 4, turn, sk next 4 sts, sl st in each of next 4 sts, turn, ch 4, (3-dtr cl, ch 4) 3 times in next ch-4 sp, sk next 2 sts on last rnd of prev motif, sl st in next 3 sts, turn.

Row 2: 8 dc in each ch-4 sp across, sk next st on last rnd of prev motif, sl st in next st, turn.

Motif 3

Row 1: Sl st in each of next 14 sts, ch 4, sk next 4 sts, sl st in each of next 4 sts, turn, ch 4, (3-dtr cl, ch 4) 3 times in next ch-4 sp, sk next 2 sts on last row of prev motif, sl st in next 3 sts, turn.

Row 2: 8 dc in each ch-4 sp across, sk next st on last row of prev motif, sl st in next st, turn.

Rep Motif 3 for desired length.

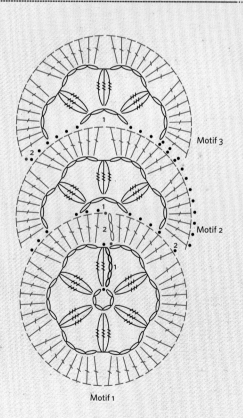

Motif 3

Motif 2

Motif 1

Pleats

✿ Multiple of 18 sts for each pleat, reducing to multiple of 6 sts for pleated fabric.

✿ Swatch: Ch 18 × 3 = 54 sts.

Ch 56 for edging as shown.

Row 1: Dc in 3rd ch from hook and in each ch across, turn—54 dc.

Rows 2–5: Ch 3 (counts as dc here and throughout), dc in each st across, turn.

Row 6: *Starting on right-hand side, fold fabric accordion fashion, folding to the back after 6 sts, then folding to the front after next 6 sts, working through triple thickness, sl st through first, 12th, and 13th st, ch 3, dc through 2nd, 11th, and 14th st, dc through 3rd, 10th, and 15th st, dc through 4th, 9th, and 16th st, dc through 5th, 8th, and 17th st, dc through 6th, 7th, and 18th st; rep from * across for length of fabric, turn—18 dc.

Row 7: Ch 3, dc in each st across—18 dc.

Rep Row 7 for desired length. Fasten off.

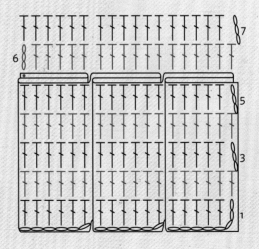

Pleated Motifs

* Multiple of 3 motifs; multiple of 17 sts across top of motifs.
→ **Note:** *Make a strip of motifs 3 times the length you need. This works for any motif.*

Instructions are for motif used in swatch as shown.

Motif 1

Ch 5, sl st in first ch to form ring.

Rnd 1: Ch 3 (counts as dc here and throughout), 15 dc in ring, sl st in top of beg ch-3 to join.

Rnd 2: Ch 3, dc in same st, 2 dc in each of next 2 sts, *(3 dc, ch 3, 3 dc) in next st, 2 dc in each of next 3 sts; rep from * 2 more times, (3 dc, ch 3, 3 dc) in next st, sl st in top of beg ch-3 to join.

Motif 2

Rnd 1: Rep Rnd 1 of Motif 1.

Rnd 2: Ch 3 (counts as dc), dc in same st, 2 dc in each of next 2 sts, (3 dc, ch 1, sl st in adjacent ch-3 sp on Motif 1, 3 dc) in next st, 2 dc in next st, (dc, sl st in adjacent motif, dc) in next st, 2 dc in next st, (3 dc, ch 1, sl st in adjacent ch-3 sp on Motif 1, 3 dc) in next st, *2 dc in each of next 3 sts, (3 dc, ch 3, 3 dc) in next st; rep from * once more, sl st in top of beg ch-3 to join.

Rep Motif 2 until you have triple the motifs as your desired length. For example, if your desired length of fabric is 10 motifs, make and join 30 motifs, because after the folds and pleats the length of the fabric will reduce to ⅓ its original size.

Assembly

Row 1: *Fold motifs in accordion fashion as foll: starting at right-hand side of motif strip, fold 2nd motif to back of first motif, then fold 3rd motif toward front, working through all three thicknesses, sl st in corner st of all 3 motifs, ch 3, dc in each st across, dc in corner sp**, dc in next corner sp; rep from * across, ending last rep at **, turn.

Row 2: Ch 3, dc in each st across, turn.

Rep Row 2 for desired length. Fasten off.

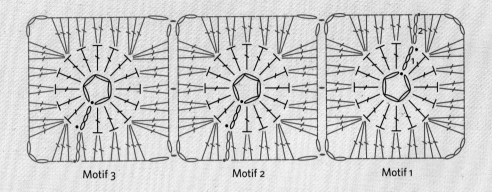

Motif 3 Motif 2 Motif 1

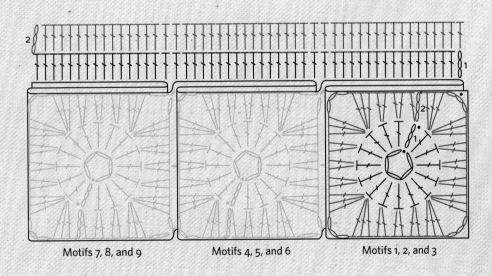

Motifs 7, 8, and 9 Motifs 4, 5, and 6 Motifs 1, 2, and 3

Mini-disc Motif

✿ Creates a fabric with a multiple of 8 + 1 sts.

→ **Note:** *Make a strip of motifs to the desired length of edging. It will become a bottom-up edging.*

Motif 1

Ch 5, sl st in 5th ch from hook to form ring, ch 3 (counts as dc), 15 dc in ring, sl st in top of ch-3 at beg of rnd to join. Fasten off.

Motif 2

Ch 5, sl st in 5th ch from hook to form ring, ch 3 (counts as dc), dc in ring, sl st in adjacent dc on prev motif, work 14 additional dc in ring, sl st in top of ch-3 at beg of rnd to join. Fasten off.

Motif 3

Ch 5, sl st in 5th ch from hook to form ring, ch 3 (counts as dc), dc in ring, sl st in 8th dc from sl st join on prev motif, work 14 additional dc in ring, sl st in top of ch-3 at beg of rnd to join. Fasten off.

Rep Motif 3 until edging is desired length.

Row 1: With RS facing, join yarn with sl st in 8th dc from first sl st join, ch 4 (counts as tr), *dc in next st, hdc in next st, sc in next 3 sts, hdc in next st, dc in next st, tr under sl st join between motifs; rep from * across, but on last rep, work tr in next st on last motif. Fasten off.

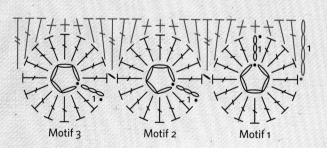

Motif 3   Motif 2   Motif 1

Diamond Motif

✿ Creates a fabric with a multiple of 10 + 1 sts.

→ **Note:** *Make a strip of motifs to the desired length of edging. It will become a bottom-up edging.*

Motif 1

Ch 5, sl st in 5th ch from hook to form ring, ch 3 (counts as dc), 2 dc in ring, (ch 3, 3 dc) 3 times in ring, ch 3, sl st in top of beg ch-3 to join. Fasten off.

Motif 2

Ch 5, sl st in 5th ch from hook to form ring, ch 3 (counts as dc), 2 dc in ring, ch 1, sl st in adjacent motif's ch-3 sp, ch 1, (3 dc, ch 3) 3 times in ring, sl st in top of beg ch-3 to join. Fasten off.

Motif 3

Ch 5, sl st in 5th ch from hook to form ring, ch 3 (counts as dc), 2 dc in ring, ch 1, sl st in ch-3 sp on adjacent motif on opposite side of previous join, ch 1), in ring work (3 dc, ch 3) 3 times in ring, sl st in top of beg ch-3 to join. Fasten off.

Rep Motif 3 until edging is desired length.

Row 1: With RS facing, join yarn with sl st in side ch-3 sp of first motif, ch 6 (counts as dc, ch 3), 3 sc in next ch-3 sp, ch 3, *dc under join between motifs, ch 3, 3 sc in next ch-3 sp, ch 3; rep from * across, dc in last ch-3 sp.

Row 2: Ch 1, sc in first dc, *3 sc in next ch-3 sp, sc in next 3 sc, 3 sc in next ch-3 sp, sc in next dc; rep from * across, turn.

Row 3: Ch 1, sc in each sc across, turn.

Rep Row 3 for desired length. Fasten off.

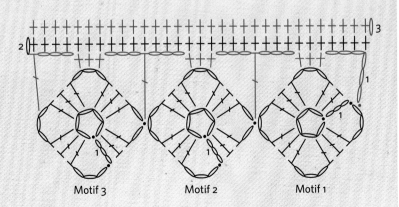

Motif 3   Motif 2   Motif 1

8-point Star Motif

✿ Creates a fabric with a multiple of 18 + 1 sts.

→ **Note:** *Make a strip of motifs to the desired length of edging. It will become a bottom-up edging.*

Instructions are written for "seamless crochet" technique. Can be modified for regular motif assembly.

Motif 1

Ch (5 + 4) = 9, sl st in 5th ch from hook to form ring.

Rnd 1: Sl st in each of next 4 ch (counts as first half of 2-tr cl), tr in ring, (ch 4, 2-tr cl in ring) 7 times, ch 4, sl st in top of ch-4 at beg of rnd.

Rnd 2: Ch 1, sc in same st, *ch 3, 3-dc cl in next ch-4 sp, ch 3 picot, ch 3, sc in next 2-tr cl; rep from * 3 more times, ch 3, 3-dc cl in next ch-4 sp, turn, leaving rem motif unworked at this point.

Motifs 2–4

Ch (5 + 4 + 1 + 3 + 3) = 16, sl st in 5th ch from hook to form ring.

Rnd 1: Rep Rnd 1 of First Motif.

Rnd 2: Sl st in next beg ch (counts as sc), ch 3, 3-dc cl in next ch-4 sp, ch 1, sl st in ch-3 picot on prev motif, ch 1, sl st in first ch (joining ch-3 picot), ch 3, sc in next cl on current motif, *ch 3, 3-dc cl in next ch-4 sp, ch-3 picot, ch 3, sc in next cl; rep from * 2 more times, ch 3, 3-dc cl in next ch-4 sp, turn, leaving rem motif unworked at this point.

Motif 5

Ch (5 + 4 + 1 + 3 + 3) = 16, sl st in 5th ch from hook to form ring.

Rnd 1: Rep Rnd 1 of First Motif.

Rnd 2: Sl st in next beg ch (counts as sc), ch 3, 3-dc cl in next ch-4 sp, ch 1, sl st in ch-3 picot on adjacent motif, ch 1, sl st in first ch (joining ch-3 picot), ch 3, sc in next cl, *ch 3, 3-dc cl in next

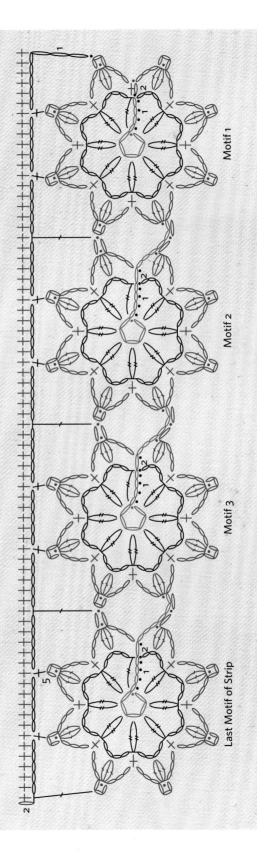

Motif 1

Motif 2

Motif 3

Last Motif of Strip

❊ tip

These gorgeous star motifs are beautiful on their own, but so boldly geometric and exquisite as an edging, whether you want to grace the edges of a formal shawl or luxurious afghan. Imagine making tiers of the motifs with bands of single crochet and overlapping them for an amazing skirt hem or scarf edge.

ch-4 sp, ch-3 picot, ch 3, sc in next cl; rep from * 5 more times.

Working across incomplete motifs, ch 3, 3-dc cl in next ch-4 sp, sl st in 3rd ch of beg ch, ch 1, sk 1 ch, sl st in next ch, ch 1, sl st in top of 3-dc cl on next motif, ch 3, sc in next cl, (ch 3, 3-dc cl in next ch-4 sp, ch-3 picot, ch 3, sc in next cl) twice; rep from * across to last motif, ch 3, 3-dc cl in next ch-4 sp, ch-3 picot, ch 3, join with sl st in first sc. Fasten off.

Row 1: With RS facing, join yarn in 4th picot from join on first motif, ch 8 (counts as dc, ch 5), sc in next picot, ch 5, sc in next picot, ch 5, dc in next junction bet motifs, *[ch 5, sc in next picot] twice, ch 5, dc in next junction bet motifs; rep from * across, ending with dc in last picot.

Row 2: Ch 1, sc in first st, *5 sc in next ch-5 sp, sc in next st; rep from * across, turn.

Rep Row 2 for desired length of fabric. Fasten off.

Hexagon Motif

✿ Creates a fabric with a multiple of 18 + 1 sts.

→ **Note:** *Make a strip of motifs to the desired length of edging. It will become a bottom-up edging.*

Motif 1

Ch 6, sl st in 6th ch from hook to form ring.

Rnd 1: Ch 3 (counts as dc here and throughout), 2 dc in ring, [ch 3, 3 dc in ring] 5 times, ch 1, hdc in top of beg ch-3 to join (counts as ch-3 sp).

Rnd 2: Ch 3, 2 dc in first sp, *(3 dc, ch 3, 3 dc) in next ch-3 sp; rep from * 4 more times, 3 dc in last ch-3 sp, ch 1, hdc in top of beg ch-3 to join (counts as ch-3 sp).

Rnd 3: Ch 3, 2 dc in first sp, *sk next 3 dc, 3 dc in sp before next dc, (3 dc, ch 3, 3 dc) in next ch-3 sp; rep from * 4 more times, sk 3 sts, 3 dc in sp before next st, 3 dc in last sp, ch 3, join with sl st in top of beg ch-3. Fasten off.

Motif 2

Rnds 1–2: Rep Rnds 1–2 of Motif 1.

Rnd 3: Ch 3, 2 dc in first sp, *sk next 3 dc, 3 dc in sp before next dc, (3 dc, ch 1, sl st in ch-3 sp of adjacent motif, ch 1, 3 dc) in next ch-3 sp; rep from * once more, **sk next 3 sts, 3 dc in sp before next st, (3 dc, ch 3, 3 dc) in next ch-3 sp; rep from ** twice, sk next 3 dc, 3 dc in sp before next dc, 3 dc in last sp, ch 3, sl st in top of beg ch-3 to join. Fasten off.

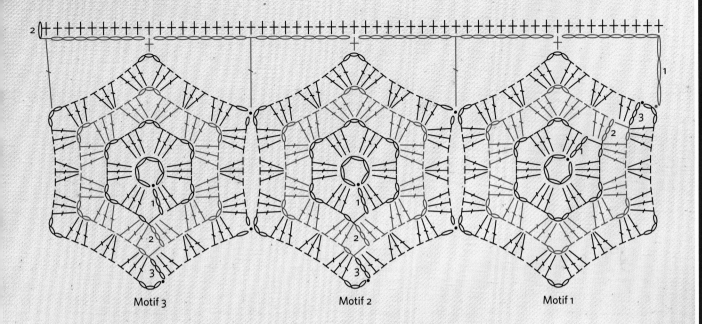

Motif 3   Motif 2   Motif 1

Rep Motif 2, joining motifs to opposite side of previous motif, until edging is desired length.

Row 1: With RS facing, join yarn with sl st in 2nd ch-3 sp to the right of 2nd join on first motif, ch 11 (counts as dc, ch 8), sc in next ch-3 sp, ch 8, dc in join between motifs, *ch 8, sc in next ch-3 sp, ch 8, dc in join between motifs; rep from * across, ending with dc in last ch-3 sp, turn.

Row 2: Ch 1, sc in first st, *8 sc in next ch-8 sp, sc in next st; rep from * across, turn.

Row 3: Ch 1, sc in each sc across, turn.

Rep Row 3 until fabric is desired length.

Fasten off.

✴tip

If you've ever made a granny square, this edging is a super simple segue into other motif shapes, since it is a granny square with 6 repeats (corners) instead of 4! The border fabric is evenly spaced and leveled by adjusting the height of the joining stitches to create a level edge on an otherwise scalloped edge.

Projects

Ephesus COWL

I chose this yarn specifically because the deep sapphire blues and emerald greens remind me of the time I lived on the Mediterranean Sea. When I look at this cowl, I can't help but reminisce about the waves crashing along the shore. The delicate nature of this yarn is beautifully emphasized with a dainty flower-petal edging. The strip of edging is wrapped into a loop and spiral-joined together to create a fabric by attaching the center flower petal to the center flower petal of the previous loop of edging. It is a seamless project that is much simpler to crochet than it looks.

MATERIALS

Yarn: Malabrigo Lace (100% merino; 470 yd [430 m] per 50 g [1.76 oz]); 137 emerald blue, 1 skein.

Hook: E/4 (3.5 mm) or size needed to obtain gauge.

GAUGE

6 rows in pattern = 4" (10 cm). First Strip = about 2½" (6.5 cm) wide.

FINISHED SIZE

18" (46 cm) wide × 13" (33 cm) deep.

Notes

❋ Pattern is based on side-to-side edging Tr Shell with 3-petal Flower on Sides (see page 51).

❋ Cowl is made by working first strip following complete edging pattern. Remainder of cowl is worked in a continuous strip that has a flower on the left side only and joins to the center flower petal on the previous strip.

First Strip

Ch 4.

Row 1: (3 tr, ch 2, 4 tr) in 4th ch from hook, ch 5, sl st in 5th ch from hook to form ring.

Row 2: (Ch 3, dc, ch 3, sl st) 3 times in ch-5 sp, ch 3, sk next 4 tr, sl st in next ch-2 sp.

Row 3: Ch 4 (counts as tr here and throughout), (3 tr, ch 3, 4 tr) in same ch-2 sp, ch 5, sl st in 5th ch from hook to form ring.

Rep Rows 2–3 for patt until strip measures 36" (91.5 cm) long ending with Row 2 of pattern and an odd number of shell rows.

Second Strip

Fold first strip in half with WS facing up.

Row 1: Ch 4, (3 tr, ch 3, 4 tr) in same ch-2 sp, ch 5, sl st in 5th ch from hook to form ring.

Row 2: (Ch 3, dc, ch 3, sl st) in ch-5 sp, (ch 3, dc, sl st in ch at base of Row 1 of First Strip, ch 3, sl st) in same ch-5 sp, (ch 3, dc, ch 3, sl st) in ch-5 sp.

Row 3: Ch 3, sk next 4 tr, sl st in next ch-2 sp, ch 4, (3 tr, ch 3, 4tr) in same ch-2 sp, ch 5, sl st in 5th ch from hook to form ring.

Row 4: (Ch 3, dc, ch 3, sl st) 3 times in ch-5 sp, ch 3, sk next 4 tr, sl st in next ch-2 sp.

Row 5: Ch 4, (3 tr, ch 3, 4 tr) in same ch-2 sp, sl st in center petal of next flower on left side of prev strip, turn.

Rep Rows 3–5 until cowl is 6 strips deep, ending with Row 5 of patt.

Last Row: Ch 3, sk next 4 tr, sl st in next ch-2 sp, (ch 3, dc, ch 3, sl st) in ch-2 sp, (ch 3, dc, sl st in center petal of next flower on left side of prev strip, ch 3, sl st) in same ch-5 sp, (ch 3, dc, ch 3, sl st) in ch-5 sp.

Fasten off and weave in loose ends.

Stitch Diagram

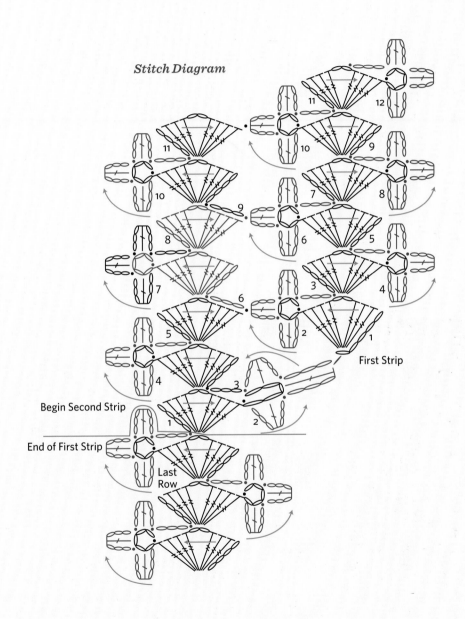

First Strip

Begin Second Strip

End of First Strip

Last
Row

Pompeii MÖBIUS

These strips of crochet fabric have a pretty flower centered in the rows. The addition of large chains at the beginning of each row is an important design feature to join the strip into a spiraling fabric. The edging is worked seamlessly right onto the Möbius in one continuous round. Using a long-striping yarn adds visual interest and mystique about the construction, but the Möbius would look gorgeous in a solid color, too.

MATERIALS

Yarn: Bernat Mosaic (100% acrylic; 209 yds [191 m] per 3.5 oz [100 g]); #44200 Ambrosia, 3 balls.

Hook: E/4 (3.5 mm) or size needed to obtain gauge.

GAUGE

13 sts and 7 rows in pattern = 3" (7.5 cm).

FINISHED SIZE

18" (45.5 cm) wide × 17" (43 cm) deep.

Note

* This pattern is based on the Flower Cut-Out Strips bottom-up edging (see page 54).

Möbius

Refer to Stitch Diagram A.

Set-up Row: Ch 6, 13 dc in 6th ch from hook.

Row 1: Ch 5, dc in each st across—13 sts.

Row 2: Ch 5 (does not count as a st), dc in first 5 dc, ch 3, sk next st, 3-dc cl in next st, ch 3, sk next st, dc in each of next 5 sts, turn.

Row 3: Ch 5 (does not count as a st), dc in first 2 dc, ch 3, 2-dc cl in side of last st worked, sk 3 sts, sc in next ch-3 sp, sc in next st, sc in next ch-3 sp, ch 3, 2-dc cl in side of last st worked, sk 3 dc, dc in each of next 2 sts, turn.

Row 4: Ch 5 (does not count as a st), dc in first 2 dc, ch 7, sk next ch-3 sp, sc in next 3 sc, ch 7, sk next ch-3 sp, dc in each of last 2 dc, turn.

Row 5: Ch 5 (does not count as a st), dc in first 2 dc, 3 dc in next ch-7 sp, sk next sc, ch 3, 3-dc cl in next sc, ch 3, sk next sc, 3 dc in next ch-7 sp, dc in each of last 2 dc, turn.

Row 6: Ch 5 (does not count as a st), dc in first 5 dc, dc in next ch-3 sp, dc in next st, dc in next ch-3 sp, dc in next 5 dc, turn.

Row 7: Ch 5, dc in each dc across, turn.

Rep Rows 2–7 until strip measures 36" long, ending with Row 7 of pattern.

Refer to assembly diagram.

To form twisted ring of Möbius, fold strip in half so Row 1 meets last row, twist Row 1 one half rotation, so that end of Row 1 meets end of last row.

Joining Rows: Rep Rows 2–7, except at the beg of each even-numbered row, replace ch 5 with the foll: (ch 2, sl st in adjacent ch-5 sp, ch 2).

Rep Joining Rows until Möbius is 4 strips wide, ending with Row 7 of pattern.

Last Row: Ch 5, dc7tog (working in every other st across row), sl st in adjacent ch-5 sp. Do not fasten off.

Edging

Refer to Stitch Diagram B.

→ **Note:** *Because a Möbius has a continuous edge, the edging is worked in 1 rnd, but completes both the top and bottom edges of the Möbius in the 1 rnd. The edging is worked back and forth on itself in 1 rnd.*

Rnd 1: Ch 1, 4 sc in same ch-5 sp, *5 sc in next ch-5 sp, ch 10, sl st in side of last sc worked, work 4 more sc in same ch-5 sp, 5 sc in next ch-5 sp, turn, 9 sc in top of last ch-10 lp, turn, 9 sc in bottom of ch-10 lp, sl st in side of last sc worked in ch-5 sp, 4 more sc in same ch-5 sp; rep from * around, sl st in first sc to join.

Fasten off and weave in loose ends.

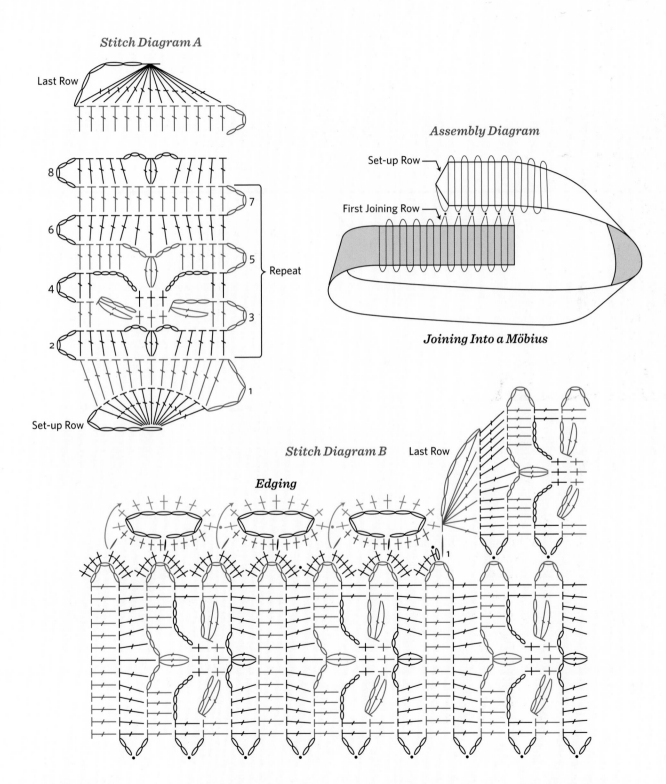

Stitch Diagram A

Last Row

8

7

6

5 Repeat

4

3

2

1

Set-up Row

Assembly Diagram

Set-up Row

First Joining Row

Joining Into a Möbius

Stitch Diagram B Last Row

Edging

1

Birka CAR COAT

Vertical stripes are an unusual crochet technique when worked in horizontal rows; experiment with them in the reversible collar of this coat. Though the technique takes a little getting used to, the reversible effect would be great for so many other projects, too! It would be fabulous for a Möbius, scarf, or shawl as well.

MATERIALS

Yarn: Naturally Caron Country (25% merino wool/75% microdenier acrylic; 3 oz [85 g] per 185 yd [170 m]); #0022 Plum Pudding (A), 9 (10, 11, 13, 14, 15, 16) balls; #0006 Berry Frappe (B), 3 (3, 4, 4, 4, 5, 5) balls.

Hook: F/5 (3.75 mm) or size needed to obtain gauge.

GAUGE

1 repeat and 4 rows = 2" (5 cm) in Body Pattern after blocking.

FINISHED SIZES

XS (S, M, L, XL, 2X, 3X).

Bust: 32 (36, 40, 44, 48, 52, 56)" (81 [91.5, 101.5, 112, 122, 132, 142] cm). *Note: This is a loose-fitting garment. Plan for about 4" ease.*

Length: 26 (26, 28, 28, 28, 28, 29)" (66 [66, 71, 71, 71, 71, 73.5] cm).

Sample shown: Size 36" (91.5 cm).

Special Stitches

Double crochet 2 together (dc2tog): [Yo, insert hook in next designated st, yo, draw yarn through st, yo, draw yarn through 2 lps on hook] twice, yo, draw yarn through 3 lps on hook.

Double crochet 4 together (dc4tog): [Yo, insert hook in next designated st, yo, draw yarn through st, yo, draw yarn through 2 lps on hook] 4 times, yo, draw yarn through 5 lps on hook.

Body Pattern (for swatch):
Refer to Stitch Diagram A.

Ch 43 (multiple of 10 + 3).

Set-up Row: Dc in 4th ch from hook, dc in next ch, *sk 2 ch, (dc, ch 3, dc) in next ch, sk 2 ch, dc in each of next 5 ch; rep from * across, ending last rep at **, dc in last 3 ch, turn—4 ch-3 sps; counts as 4 patt reps.

Row 1: Ch 3, sk next 2 sts, dc in next st (counts as dc2tog), *ch 2, 5 dc in ch-3 sp**, ch 2, sk next dc, dc2tog over next 5 sts, working first leg in next dc, sk 3 dc, work 2nd leg in next dc, complete cl; rep from * across, ending last rep at **, ch 2, sk next dc, dc2tog over last 3 sts, working first leg in next dc, sk 1 dc, work 2nd leg in next dc, complete cluster, turn.

Row 2: Ch 4 (counts as dc, ch 1), dc in first st, sk next ch-2 sp, dc in each of next 5 dc, *sk next ch-2 sp, work (dc, ch 3, dc) in sp bet 2 legs of next dc2tog, sk next ch-2 sp, dc in next 5 dc; rep from * across, ending with sk next ch-2 sp, (dc, ch 1, dc) in last st, turn.

Row 3: Ch 3, 2 dc in next ch-1 sp, *ch 2, sk next dc, dc2tog over next 5 dc, skipping center 3 dc, ch 2**, 5 dc in next ch-3 sp; rep from * across, ending last rep at **, 3 dc in last ch-1 sp, turn.

Row 4: Ch 3 (counts as dc here and throughout), dc in each of next 2 dc, *work (dc, ch 3, dc) in sp between 2 legs of next dc2tog**, dc in each of next 5 sts; rep from * across, ending last rep at **, dc in each of last 3 sts, turn.

Rep Rows 1–4 for pattern.

Stitch Diagram A

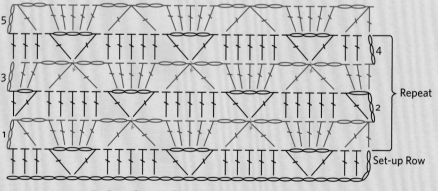

Reduced Sample of Body Pattern

Lower Body

With A, ch 203 (223, 243, 263, 283, 303, 323).

Set-up Row: Dc in 4th ch from hook, dc in next ch, *sk 2 ch, (dc, ch 3, dc) in next ch, sk 2 ch, dc in each of next 5 ch; rep from * across, ending last rep at **, dc in last 3 ch, turn—20 (22, 24, 26, 28, 30, 32) ch-3 sps; counts as 20 (22, 24, 26, 28, 30, 32) patt reps.

Work even in Body Pattern (see Special Stitches) until body measures 14 (14, 16, 16, 16, 16, 16)" from beg, ending with Row 4 of patt.

Decrease Row: Ch 3, sk next 2 sts, dc in next st (counts as dc2tog), ch 2, 5 dc in ch-3 sp, *ch 2, sk next dc, dc2tog over next 5 sts, working first leg in next dc, sk 3 dc, work 2nd leg in next dc, complete cl, ch 2, 5 dc in ch-3 sp*; rep from * to * 2 (2, 3, 3, 4, 4, 5) more times, **ch 2, dc4tog over next 2 groups of 5-dc as foll: work first leg in first dc of next group, 2nd leg in 5th dc of same group, 3rd leg in first dc of next group, 4th leg in 5th dc of same group, complete cluster**; rep from * to * 8 (10, 10, 12, 12, 14, 14) times, rep from ** to ** once; rep from * to * 4 (4, 5, 5, 6, 6, 7) times, ch 2, dc2tog worked over last 3 sts, skipping center st, turn—16 (18, 20, 22, 24, 26, 28) ch-3 sps; counts as 16 (18, 20, 22, 24, 26, 28) patt reps.

Starting with Row 2 of patt, work even in est Body Pattern for 9 more rows, ending with Row 2 of patt.

Separate for Front and Back

Left Front

Row 1: Ch 3, 2 dc in next ch-1 sp, ch 2, sk next dc, dc2tog over next 5 dc, skipping center 3 dc, ch 2, *5 dc in next ch-3 sp, ch 2, sk next dc, dc2tog over next 5 dc, skipping center 3 dc, ch 2; rep from * 2 (2, 3, 3, 4, 4) more times, 3 dc in next ch-3 sp, turn, leaving rem sts unworked—4 (4, 5, 5, 6, 6, 7) patt reps.

Rows 2–3: Starting with Row 3 of patt, work even in est Body Pattern on 4 (4, 5, 5, 6, 6, 7) patt reps.

Shape Neck

Row 4: Work in Row 2 of patt across to last group of 5 dc, sk next ch-2 sp, dc in last st (dec made), turn.

Row 5: Ch 3, sk next 4 dc, dc in next st (counts as dc2tog) (dec made), ch 2, *5 dc in next ch-3 sp, ch 2, dc2tog in (next st, sk 3 sts, and next st), ch 2; rep from * 2 (2, 3, 3, 4, 4, 5) more times, 2 dc in next ch-1 sp, dc in last st, turn.

Starting with Row 2 of patt, work even in est Body Pattern for 3 (3, 3, 5, 5, 5, 7) rows. Fasten off.

Back

With WS facing, sk 7 dc to the left of Row 1 of Left Front, join A with sl st in next ch-3 sp.

Row 1: Ch 3 (counts as dc), 2 dc in same sp, *ch 2, dc2tog over next 5 dc, skipping center 3 dc, ch 2**, 5 dc in next ch-3 sp; rep from * 6 (8, 8, 10, 10, 12, 12) more times; rep from * to ** once, 3 dc in next ch-3 sp, turn, leaving rem sts unworked—8 (10, 10, 12, 12, 14, 14) pattern reps.

Starting with Row 4 of patt, work even in est Body Pattern until Back measures same as finished Left Front. Fasten off.

Right Front

With WS facing, sk 7 dc to the left of Row 1 of Left Front, join A with sl st in next ch-3 sp.

Row 1: Ch 3, 2 dc in same sp, *ch 2, sk next dc, dc2tog over next 5 dc, skipping center 3 dc, ch 2**, 5 dc in next ch-3 sp; rep from * 2 (2, 3, 3, 4, 4, 6) more times, rep from * to ** once, ch 2, 3 dc in last ch-1 sp, turn.

Rows 2–3: Rep Rows 2–3 of Left Front.

Row 4: Ch 3 (counts as dc), sk next ch-2 sp, dc in each of next 5 dc (dec made), *sk next ch-2 sp, work (dc, ch 3, dc) in sp bet 2 legs of next dc2tog, sk next ch-2 sp, dc in next 5 dc; rep from * across, ending with sk next ch-2 sp, (dc, ch 1, dc) in last st, turn.

Row 5: Work in Row 3 of Body Pattern across to last group of 5 dc, ending with ch 2, dc2tog over last 6 sts, skipping center 4 dc (dec made), turn.

Row 6: Ch 3 (counts as dc), sk next ch-2 sp (dec made), dc in each of next 5 sts, *work (dc, ch 3, dc) in sp between 2 legs of next dc2tog**, dc in each of next 5 sts; rep from * across, ending last rep at **, dc in each of last 3 sts, turn.

Row 6: Work in Row 4 of patt across to last group of 5 dc, ending with sk next ch-2 sp, dc in sp under dc2tog on prev row (dec made), turn.

Row 7: Ch 3, sk next 4 sts, dc in next st (counts as dc2tog) (dec made), ch 2, 5 dc in next ch-3 sp, ch 2, *dc2tog over next 5 dc, skipping center 3 dc, ch 2, 5 dc in next ch-3 sp, ch 2; rep from * across, ending with dc2tog over last 3 sts, skipping center st, turn.

Row 8: Work in Row 2 of patt across to last group of 5 dc, sk next ch-2 sp, dc in sp bet 2 legs of last dc2tog (dec made), turn.

Rows 9–11: Rep Rows 5–7 of Shape Neck—2 (2, 3, 3, 4, 4, 5) pattern reps.

Row 7: Work in Row 1 of Body Pattern across to last group of 5 dc, ending with ch 2, dc2tog over last 6 sts, skipping center 4 dc (dec made), turn.

Row 8: Ch 4 (counts as dc, ch 1), dc in first st, sk next ch-2 sp, dc in each of next 5 dc, *sk next ch-2 sp, work (dc, ch 3, dc) in sp bet 2 legs of next dc2tog, sk next ch-2 sp, dc in next 5 dc; rep from * across, ending with sk next ch-2 sp, (dc, ch 1, dc) in last st, turn.

Ch 3, sk next ch-2 sp, dc in each of next 5 dc, *sk next ch-2 sp, work (dc, ch 3, dc) in sp between 2 legs of next dc2tog, sk next ch-2 sp, dc in each of next 5 dc; rep from across, ending with sk next ch-2 sp, (dc, ch 1, dc) in last st.

Rows 9–11: Rep Rows 5–7 of Shape Neck—2 (2, 3, 3, 4, 4, 5) pattern reps.

Starting with Row 2 of patt, work even in est Body Pattern for 3 (3, 3, 5, 5, 5, 7) rows. Fasten off.

Assembly

With RS facing, sew Front to Back at shoulders.

Sleeves

→ **Note:** *Sleeves are worked in joined rnds of Body Pattern. To maintain look of body, turn at the end of each rnd.*

With WS facing, join A with sl st in center dc at under arm of one sleeve opening.

Sizes S, M, and L Only

Rnd 1 (WS): Ch 3, dc in next 2 dc, (dc, ch 3, dc) in next ch-3 sp, working across row-end sts, *3 dc in next row-end dc, 2 dc in next row-end st, (dc, ch 3, dc) in top of next row-end st, sk next row-end st*; rep from * to * twice, 3 dc in next row-end dc, 2 dc in next row-end st, ch 3, sc in shoulder seam, rep from * to * 3 times, 3 dc in next row-end dc, 2 dc in next row-end st, ch 3, sc in next ch-3 sp, dc in next 2 dc of underarm, sl st in top of beg ch-3 to join, turn—8 patt reps.

Sizes XL, 2X, and 3X Only

Rnd 1 (WS): Ch 3, dc in next 2 dc, (dc, ch 3, dc) in next ch-3 sp, working across row-end sts, *3 dc in next row-end dc, 2 dc in next row-end st, (dc, ch 3, dc) in top of next row-end st, sk next row-end st*; rep from * to * twice, [3 dc in next row-end dc, 2 dc in next row-end st, (dc, ch 3, dc) in next row-end dc] twice; rep from * to * 3 times, 3 dc in next row-end dc, 2 dc in next row-end st, (dc, ch 3, dc) in next row-end dc, dc in next 2 dc of underarm, sl st in top of beg ch-3 to join, turn— 9 patt reps.

All Sizes

Rnd 2: Ch 3, dc in each of next 2 dc, *work (dc, ch 3, dc) in sp between 2 legs of next dc2tog**, dc in each of next 5 sts; rep from * around, ending last rep at **, dc in each of last 2 sts, turn—8 (8, 8, 9, 9, 9) patt reps.

Rnd 3: Ch 3, sk 2 sts, dc in next st (counts as dc2tog), *ch 2, 5 dc in ch-3 sp, ch 2, sk next dc**, dc2tog over next 5 sts, skipping center 3 dc; rep from * around, ending last rep at **, dc in next dc, sk 1 dc, sl st in first dc to join, turn.

Rnd 4: Ch 4 (counts as dc, ch 1), dc in first st, *sk next ch-2 sp, dc in each of next 5 dc, sk next ch-2 sp**, work (dc, ch 3, dc) in sp bet 2 legs of next dc2tog; rep from * around, ending last rep at **, dc in first st, ch 1, sl st in top of beg ch-3 to join, turn.

Rnd 5: Ch 3, 2 dc in next ch-1 sp, *ch 2, sk next dc, dc2tog over next 5 dc, skipping center 3 dc, ch 2**, 5 dc in next ch-3 sp; rep from * across, ending last rep at **, 2 dc in last ch-1 sp, sl st in top of beg ch-3 to join, turn.

Rep Rows 2–5 until sleeve measures 15 (16, 16, 17, 17, 17)" from beg or 1" less than desired length.

Last Row: Ch 1, (sc, ch 3, 3-dc cl) in first st, *sk next 3 sts, (sc, ch 3, 3-dc cl) in next st; rep from * around, join with sl st in first sc. Fasten off.

Rep in other armhole opening for 2nd sleeve.

Collar Half (make 2)

→ **Note:** *Collar is worked using side-to-side Reversible Interlocking Vertical Stripes edging (see page 62).*

Starting at bottom edge, with A, ch 28.

Row 1: 2 dc in 4th ch from hook, ch 3, sk next 7 ch, *(2 dc, ch 1, 2 dc) in next ch, ch 3, sk 7 ch; rep from *

across to last ch, 3 dc in last ch, drop A to be picked up later, do not turn.

Row 2: With RS facing, join B with sl st in top of ch-3 at beg of last row, *ch 3, working over ch-3 sp, sk next 3 ch sts in foundation ch 2 rows below, (2 dc, ch 1, 2 dc) in next ch; rep from * across, ending with ch 1, hdc in top of last dc, turn.

Row 3: Pick up A, ch 3 (counts as dc), 2 dc in same st, *ch 3, working over ch-3 sp in last row, (2 dc, ch 1, 2 dc) in same color ch-1 sp 2 rows below; rep from * across, ending with ch 3, 3 dc in top of ch-3 2 rows below, drop B to be picked up later, do not turn.

Row 4: Pick up B, ch 3 (working the first ch around the color B ch-3 to bring yarn to front), *working over ch-3 sp in last row, (2 dc, ch 1, 2 dc) in same color ch-1 sp 2 rows below, ch 3; rep from * across, ending with ch 1, hdc in top of last dc, turn.

Rep Rows 3–4 until collar measures 36" (91.5 cm) from beg or the length of front edge plus half of back neck edge, ending each half with same row of patt. Aligning bottom edge of one Half Collar with bottom edge of Right Front, using A, sew left side of Collar to right front edge, and across first half of back neck edge. Sew other Half Collar to Left Front edge and other half of back neck edge. With A, sew Collar Halves tog across last rows.

Belt

Row 1: Ch 4 (counts as tr, here and throughout), 3 tr in 4th ch from hook, turn.

Row 2: Sl st in sp between 2nd and 3rd sts, ch 4, 3 tr in same sp, turn.

Rep Row 2 until belt measures 76" (193 cm) or desired length, sl st in sp between 2nd and 3rd sts. Fasten off. Weave in loose ends.

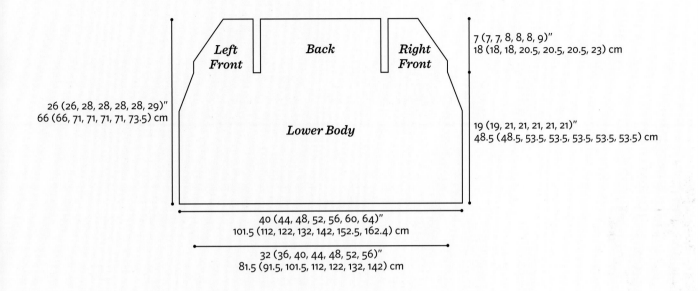

Left Front Back Right Front

7 (7, 7, 8, 8, 8, 9)"
18 (18, 18, 20.5, 20.5, 20.5, 23) cm

26 (26, 28, 28, 28, 28, 29)"
66 (66, 71, 71, 71, 71, 73.5) cm

Lower Body

19 (19, 21, 21, 21, 21, 21)"
48.5 (48.5, 53.5, 53.5, 53.5, 53.5, 53.5) cm

40 (44, 48, 52, 56, 60, 64)"
101.5 (112, 122, 132, 142, 152.5, 162.4) cm

32 (36, 40, 44, 48, 52, 56)"
81.5 (91.5, 101.5, 112, 122, 132, 142) cm

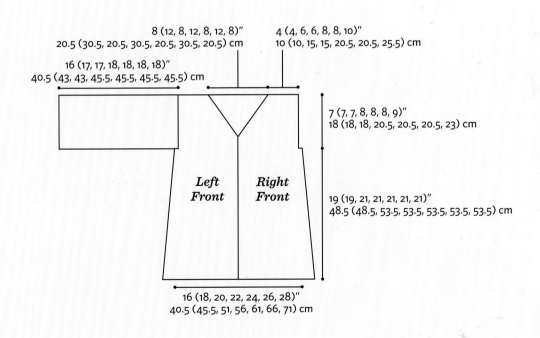

8 (12, 8, 12, 8, 12, 8)"
20.5 (30.5, 20.5, 30.5, 20.5, 30.5, 20.5) cm

4 (4, 6, 6, 8, 8, 10)"
10 (10, 15, 15, 20.5, 20.5, 25.5) cm

16 (17, 17, 18, 18, 18, 18)"
40.5 (43, 43, 45.5, 45.5, 45.5, 45.5) cm

7 (7, 7, 8, 8, 8, 9)"
18 (18, 18, 20.5, 20.5, 20.5, 23) cm

Left Front Right Front

19 (19, 21, 21, 21, 21, 21)"
48.5 (48.5, 53.5, 53.5, 53.5, 53.5, 53.5) cm

16 (18, 20, 22, 24, 26, 28)"
40.5 (45.5, 51, 56, 61, 66, 71) cm

Birka Car Coat

Luxor BLANKET

The center rectangle of this blanket is very simple to crochet in rounds. The outer edging complements that simplicity with an unusual shape and texture that becomes even more interesting by manipulating it around the blanket's corners to create a frame. Instead of joining as you go or sewing on a completed edging, use the addition of a third contrast color in the pretty spike edging to simultaneously add a spark of color and texture while joining the outer edge to the center blanket.

MATERIALS

Yarn: Vickie Howell Sheep(ish) Worsted Roving Yarn by Caron (70% acrylic/30% wool; 167 yd [153 m] per 3 oz [85 g]); #0011 Taupe(ish) (A), 9 balls; #0020 Chartreuse(ish) (B), 5 balls; #0016 Teal(ish) (C), 1 ball.

Hook: H/8 (5 mm) or size needed to obtain gauge.

Notions: 4 stitch markers.

GAUGE

13 sts and 8 rows = 4" (10 cm) in dc. Gauge is not critical for this project.

FINISHED SIZE

44" × 69" (112 × 175 cm).

Spike tr2tog: *Yo twice, insert hook in specified st 2 rows below, pull up a lp elongating yarn until you are at the top of current row, (yo, pull through 2 lps) 2 times; rep from * once, yo, pull through all 3 lps on hook.

Spike tr3tog: *Yo twice, insert hook in specified st 2 rows below, pull up a lp elongating yarn until you are at the top of current row, (yo, pull through 2 lps) 2 times; rep from * 2 more times, yo, pull through all 4 lps on hook.

Stitch Diagram A

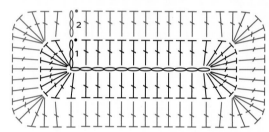

Reduced Sample of Center Rectangle Pattern

Blanket

Center Rectangle

Refer to Stitch Diagram A.

With A, ch 83.

Rnd 1: 10 dc in 4th ch from hook, dc in each ch across to last ch, 11 dc in last ch, working in opposite side of foundation ch, dc in each ch across, sl st in top of beg ch-3 to join—178 dc.

Rnd 2: Ch 3 (counts as dc here and throughout), dc in next st, 5 dc in next st (place marker in center dc), dc in each of next 5 sts, 5 dc in next st (place marker in center dc), dc in each of next 82 sts, 5 dc

in next st (place marker in center dc), dc in each of next 5 sts, 5 dc in next st (place marker in center dc), dc in each st to beg of rnd, sl st in top of beg ch-3 to join—194 dc; 86 dc between markers on long side; 9 dc between markers on short side. *Note: Move marker up to center dc of each 5-dc corner in each rnd.*

Rnds 3–31: Ch 3, *dc in each dc to next marker, 5 dc in next marked st; rep from * around, dc in each st to beg of rnd, join with sl st in top of beg ch-3—658 dc; 202 dc bet markers on long side; 116 dc between markers on short side. *Note: This increases each rnd by 16 sts.*

Fasten off.

Overlapping Circles Edging

Refer to Stitch Diagram B.

→ **Note:** *Uses miscellaneous Faux Overlapping Circle Motifs edging (see page 72). Edging is worked separately from blanket. With the use of a third color and a third edging, this border will be joined to the center rectangle at the end.*

Motif 1

→ **Note:** *The first motif is worked in rnds, but all rem motifs are worked in rows. For consistency, turn your work after each rnd on first motif so the fabric alternates RS and WS like all rem motifs.*

Ch 4, sl st in 4th ch from hook to form ring.

Rnd 1 (RS): Ch 3 (counts as dc here and throughout), 11 dc in ring, sl st in top of beg ch-3 to join, turn—12 dc.

Rnd 2 (WS): Ch 3, dc in first st, 2 dc in each st around, sl st in top of beg ch-3 to join, turn—24 dc.

Rnd 3 (RS): Ch 3, dc in first st, dc in next st, *2 dc in next st, dc in next st; rep from * around, sl st in top of beg ch-3 to join, turn—36 dc.

Rnd 4 (WS): Ch 3, dc in first st, dc in next 2 sts, *2 dc in next st, dc in next 2 sts; rep from * around, sl st in top of beg ch-3 to join, do not turn—48 dc.

Motif 2

Row 1: Ch 4, sk next 2 sts, sl st in each of next 3 sts on last rnd of last motif, turn, 9 dc in ch-4 sp, sk 1 st on last rnd of last motif, sl st in each of next 3 sts, turn.

Row 2: 2 dc in each st across, sk 1 st on last rnd of last motif, sl st in each of next 3 sts, turn.

Row 3: *2 dc in next st, dc in next st; rep from * across, sk 1 st on last rnd of last motif, sl st in each of next 3 sts, turn.

Row 4: *2 dc in next st, dc in each of next 2 sts; rep from * across, sk 1 st on last rnd of last motif, sl st in next st, turn.

Motif 3

Sl st in each of next 17 sts. Rep Rows 2–4 of Motif 2.

Motifs 4–20

Rep Motif 3.

Motif 21

Refer to Stitch Diagram C.

Sl st in each of next 8 sts for 90-degree turn. Rep Motif 2.

Motifs 22–33

Rep Motif 3.

Motif 34

Sl st in each of next 26 sts for 90-degree turn.

Motifs 35–55

Rep Motif 3.

Motif 56

Rep Motif 34.

Motifs 57–69

Rep Motif 3. Fasten off.

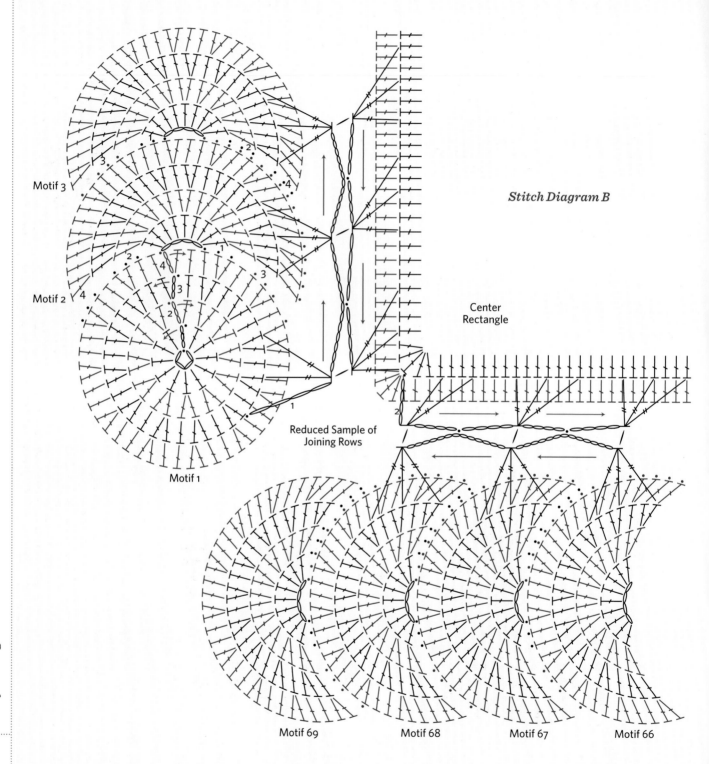

Motif 3

Motif 2

Motif 1

Stitch Diagram B

Center
Rectangle

Reduced Sample of
Joining Rows

Motif 69

Motif 68

Motif 67

Motif 66

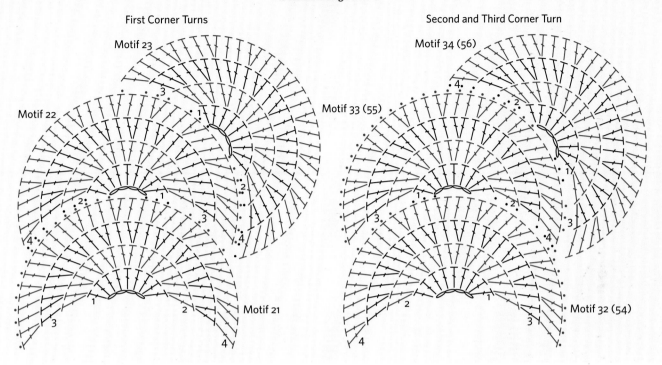

Stitch Diagram C

First Corner Turns

Motif 23

Motif 22

Motif 21

Second and Third Corner Turn

Motif 34 (56)

Motif 33 (55)

Motif 32 (54)

Starburst Joining Edging

→ **Note:** *This section is worked in 2 parts. First, work a row of sts on the interior edge (inside the corners) of the overlapping circles edging. Then, work a row of sts on the exterior edge of the rectangle, while at the same time joining to the first row of starburst edging worked on the circles.*

Row 1: With RS facing, working on interior edge of Motif 1, working in tops of sts in Rnd 3, starting at dc 2 rows below sl st joining Motif 2 to Motif 1, sk next 5 sts to the right, join C with sl st in next in next dc in Rnd 3 of Motif 1 (see diagram), ch 4 (counts as leg of tr3tog), sk next 2 sts, work spike tr2tog (see Special Stitches) working first leg in next st, sk next 2 sts, work next leg in next st, complete tr2tog, *ch 13, in Row 3 of next motif, work spike tr3tog (see Special Stitches) in first, 4th and 7th dc (skipping 2 sts between each spike); rep from * across to Motif 68. Fasten off, leaving last motif unworked.

Line up outer edging next to rectangle. As you crochet the foll row onto the outer edge of the rectangle, join to the existing row of C on the outer edging.

Row 2: Join C with sl st in the right side of a short edge on the rectangular piece, working in base of sts 2 rows below, starting corner dc, work a spike tr3tog in first, 4th, 7th sts (skipping 2 sts between each spike), sl st in top of last spike tr3tog on Row 1 (Motif 68), *ch 4, sl st in next ch-13 sp on Row 1, ch 4, sk next 3 sts 2 rows below, spike tr3tog in first, 4th, and 7th sts (skipping 2 sts between each spike), sl st in top of next spike tr3tog on Row 1; rep from * across to first tr3tog in Motif 1, adjusting to position Motifs 22, 33, and 55 at the corners. Fasten off.

Overlap Motif 69 over Motif 1 to simulate the look of the other corners and sew in place. Weave in loose ends.

Anni BELT/SCARF

This is an incredibly quick project to whip up and looks so much more complicated than it really is. The overlapping coins are really just crocheted in one strip of narrow rows of partial circles, even though it looks like they're separate motifs. Wear it as a loose belt or sash or wrap it around your neck a couple times as a skinny scarf.

MATERIALS

Yarn: Bijou Basin Bijou Spun Lhasa Wilderness (75% yak, 25% bamboo; 2 oz [56 g] per 180 yd [164.5 m]); #04 blush, 1 skein.

Hook: G/6 (4 mm) or size needed to obtain gauge.

GAUGE

First motif = 2" (5 cm) in diameter after blocking.

FINISHED SIZE

2" × 82" (5 × 208 cm).

Note

❋ Pattern is based on miscellaneous edging Faux Overlapping Mini-wheel Motifs; see stitch dictionary for diagram (page 71).

Faux Overlapping Mini-wheel Motifs

Motif 1

Ch 4, sl st in 4th ch from hook to form ring.

Rnd 1 (RS): Ch 4 (counts as dc, ch 1), [dc, ch 1] 7 times in ring, sl st in 3rd ch of beg ch-4 to join, turn.

Rnd 2 (WS): Sl st in next ch-1 sp, ch 3 (counts as dc), 3 dc in same ch-1 sp, 4 dc in each ch-1 sp around, sl st in top of beg ch-3 to join.

Motif 2

Row 1: Ch 4, sk 2 sts on last rnd of prev motif, sl st in each of next 3 sts, turn, ([dc, ch 1] 5 times, dc) in next ch-4 sp, sk next 2 sts on last rnd of prev motif, sl st in each of next 3 sts, turn.

Row 2: 4 dc in each ch-1 sp across, sk next st on last rnd of prev motif, sl st in next st, turn.

Motif 3

Row 1: Sl st in each of next 9 sts on last rnd of prev motif, ch 4, sk next 2 sts, sl st in each of next 3 sts, turn, ([dc, ch 1] 5 times, dc) in next ch-4 sp, sk next 2 sts on last rnd of prev motif, sl st in each of next 3 sts, turn.

Row 2: 4 dc in each ch-1 sp across, sk next st on last rnd of prev motif, sl st in next st.

Rep Motif 3 until piece measures 82", desired length, or until you run out of yarn.

Wash, block to finished measurements, and let dry. Weave in loose ends.

Persepolis TOP

I used contrasting colors to emphasize the spiraling flower edgings applied to the front of this top, and I think it would be exquisite in more subtle colors, too. The base of the top is worked in mesh from corner to corner with diagonal increases and decreases. The ruffled edging is worked right into the base fabric, starting with the widest row from corner to corner. This technique would be fantastic on a pillow or for tiered edging along the bottom few inches of a skirt or triangular shawl.

MATERIALS

Yarn: Filatura di Crosa Zarina (100% merino superwash; 180 yd [165 m] per 1.75 oz [50 g]); #1783 Fuchsia (A), 4 (4, 5, 6, 6) balls.

Filatura di Crosa Superior (70% cashmere/25% Schappe Silk/5% extrafine merino; 330 yd [300 m] per .88 oz [25 g]); #70 Mauve (B), 1 ball.

Hook: E/4 (3.5 mm) or size needed to obtain gauge.

GAUGE

10 rows and 25 sts = 4" (10 cm).

FINISHED SIZES

XS (S, M, L, XL)

Finished bust: 34 (38, 42, 48, 52)" (86 [96.5, 106.5, 122, 132] cm).

Finished length: 19½ (20½, 22½, 22½, 22½)" (49.5 [52, 57, 57, 57] cm).

Special Stitches

Half double crochet 3 together through back loops only (hdc3tog-tbl): [Yo, insert hook in blp of next st, yo and draw up a lp] 3 times, yo, draw yarn through all lps on hook.

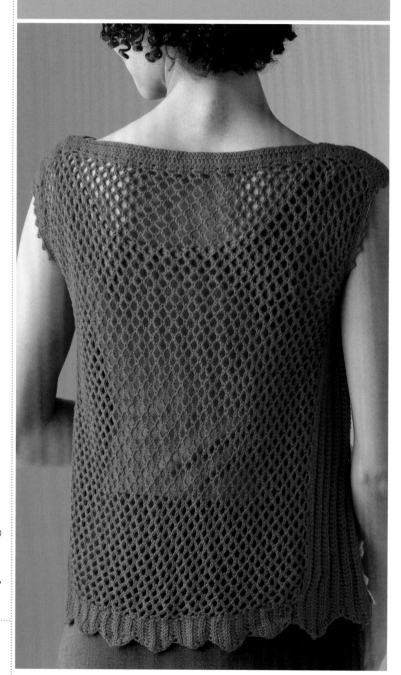

Front/Back (make 2)

Refer to Stitch Diagram A.

→ **Note:** *Front and Back are worked in diagonal rows starting in the bottom-right corner.*

Increase Corner

Row 1: With A, ch 6, dc in 6th ch from hook, turn—1 ch-2 sp.

Row 2: Ch 5, dc in first st, ch 2, sk next ch-2 sp, (dc, ch 2, dc) in 3rd ch of beg ch-6, turn—3 ch-2 sps.

Row 3: Ch 5, dc in first st, [ch 2, sk next ch-2 sp, dc in next dc] twice, ch 2, sk next 2 ch, (dc, ch 2, dc) in 3rd ch of beg ch-5, turn—5 ch-2 sps.

Row 4: Ch 5, dc in first st, [ch 2, sk next ch-2 sp, dc in next dc] 4 times, ch 2, sk next 2 ch, (dc, ch 2, dc) in 3rd ch of beg ch-5, turn—7 ch-2 sps.

Row 5: Ch 5, dc in first st, [ch 2, sk next ch-2 sp, dc in next dc] across to last ch-2 sp, ch 2, sk next 2 ch, (dc, ch 2, dc) in 3rd ch of beg ch-5, turn—9 ch-2 sps.

Rep Row 5 until piece measures 16 (18, 20, 20, 20)" from beg across each side of triangle.

Decrease corner

Row 1: (Ch 3, dc in next st) counts as dc2tog, *ch 2, sk next ch-2 sp, dc in next dc; rep from * across to last 2 ch-2 sps, ch 2, dc2tog over next dc and 3rd ch of beg ch-5, turn.

Rep last row until 3 ch-2 sps rem.

Next row: (Ch 3, dc in next st) counts as dc2tog, ch 2, dc2tog over next dc and 3rd ch of beg ch-5, turn—1 ch-2 sp.

Last row: Ch 3, sk next 2 ch, dc in 3rd ch of beg ch-5. Do not fasten off.

Top Edging

Row 1: With Row 1 on bottom right, working across top edge of piece, ch 3, 3 dc in each row-end st across, dc in corner st, turn.

Stitch Diagram A

(Ending at top-left corner)

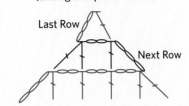

Last Row

Next Row

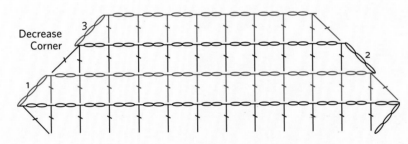

Decrease
Corner

3

1

2

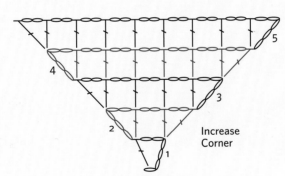

5

4

3

2

1

Increase
Corner

Front/Back
(Starting at bottom-right corner)

Five trim rows are worked diagonally across front of sweater, working in ch-2 sps from bottom-right corner to top-left corner.

First Trim Row: With RS facing, join B with sl st in first ch-2 sp of last inc row on bottom-right corner of Front, ch 6 (counts as tr, ch 2), (tr, [ch 2, tr] 4 times) in same sp, *sk next ch-2 sp, (sc, ch 5, sc) in next ch-2 sp, turn, (ch 5, sc) 3 times in ch-5 sp, turn, (sl st, ch 3, 2 dc, ch-4 picot, 2 dc, ch 3, sl st) in each of next 3 ch-5 sps, sk next ch-2 sp, (tr, [ch 2, tr] 5 times) in next ch-2 sp; rep from * across. Fasten off.

2nd and 3rd Trim Rows: Sk 3 rows above last row worked, rep First Trim Row in next row.

4th Trim Row: Sk 3 rows below First Trim Row, rep First Trim Row in next row.

5th Trim Row: Sk 3 rows below last row worked, rep First Trim Row in next row.

First Gussett

→ **Note:** *Lower edging is worked side to side while joining to the lower edge of both the front and back, while at the same time the side gussets are added to the lower edging and joined to the sides of front and back. Place a marker 7 (7½, 8, 8½, 9)" below top edge of front and back on each side for armholes.*

Sizes Small, Medium, Large Only

Row 1: With RS facing, join A in bottom-right corner of Back, ch 6, hdc in 2nd ch from hook, hdc in next 4 ch, 3 hdc in each row-end st across to marker, turn.

Row 2: Ch 1, hdc-tbl in each st across to last st, 3 hdc-tbl in last st, turn.

Row 3: Ch 1, 3 hdc-tbl in first st, hdc-tbl in each st across to last 5 sts, turn.

Row 4: Ch 1, hdc-tbl in each st across to last st, 3 hdc-tbl in last st, turn.

Row 2: Ch 3, dc in each dc across, turn.

Work 4 (1, 1, 1, 1) more rows even in dc. Fasten off.

Front Trim Rows

→ **Note:** *Front trim rows are adapted from Row 2 of top-down Superior Flower edging (see page 24).*

Row 5: Ch 1, hdc3tog-tbl (see Special Stitches) over first 3 sts, hdc-tbl in each st across to within last 5 sts, turn, leaving rem sts unworked.

Row 6: Ch 1, hdc-tbl in each st across to last 3 sts, hdc3tog-tbl over last 3 sts, turn.

Row 7: Ch 1, hdc3tog-tbl over first 3 sts, hdc-tbl in each st across to within last 5 sts, turn, leaving rem sts unworked.

Row 8: Ch 1, hdc-tbl in each st across to last st, 3 hdc-tbl in last st, turn.

Row 9: Ch 1, 3 hdc-tbl in first st, hdc-tbl in each st across, hdc-tbl of next 5 sts 2 rows below, turn.

Row 10: Ch 1, hdc-tbl in each st across to last st, 3 hdc-tbl in last st, turn.

Row 11: Ch 1, hdc3tog-tbl over first 3 sts, hdc-tbl in each st across, hdc-tbl of next 5 sts 2 rows below, turn.

Row 12: Ch 1, hdc-tbl in each st across to last 3 sts, hdc3tog-tbl over last 3 sts, turn.

Row 13: Ch 1, hdc3tog-tbl over first 3 sts, hdc-tbl in each st across, hdc-tbl of next 5 sts 2 rows below, turn.

Row 14: Ch 1, hdc-tbl in each st across to last st, 3 hdc-tbl in last st, turn.

Size X-Large and 2X-Large Only

Row 1: With RS facing, join A in bottom-right corner of Back, ch 6, hdc in 2nd ch from hook, hdc in next 4 ch, 3 hdc in each row-end st across to marker, turn.

Row 2: Ch 1, hdc-tbl in each st across to last st, 3 hdc-tbl in last st, turn.

Row 3: Ch 1, 3 hdc-tbl in first st, hdc-tbl in each st across, turn.

Row 4: Ch 1, hdc-tbl in each st across to last st, 3 hdc-tbl in last st, turn.

Row 5: Ch 1, hdc3tog-tbl (see Special Stitches) over first 3 sts, hdc-tbl in each st across, turn.

Row 6: Ch 1, hdc-tbl in each st across to last st, 3 hdc-tbl of last st, turn.

Row 7: Ch 1, hdc3tog-tbl over first 3 sts, hdc-tbl in each st across, turn.

Rows 8–13 (19): Rep Rows 2–7 once (twice).

Row 14 (20): Ch 1, hdc-tbl in each st across to last st, 3 hdc-tbl in last st, turn.

→ **Note:** *Side edge is not joined at this point.*

All Sizes

Front Bottom Edging

Row 1: Ch 1, 3 hdc-tbl in first st, hdc-tbl in each of next 7 sts, sl st in next row-end st on Front bottom edge of sweater, turn.

Row 2: Ch 1, hdc-tbl in each st across to last st, 3 hdc-tbl in last st, turn.

Row 3: Ch 1, hdc3tog-tbl over first 3 sts, hdc-tbl in each st across, sl st in next row-end st on bottom edge of sweater, turn.

Row 4: Ch 1, hdc-tbl in each st across to last st, 3 hdc-tbl in last st, turn.

Row 5: Ch 1, hdc3tog-tbl over first 3 sts, hdc-tbl in each st across, sl st in next row-end st on bottom edge of sweater, turn.

Row 6: Rep Row 2.

Row 7: Ch 1, 3 hdc-tbl in first st, hdc-tbl in each st across, sl st in next row-end st on bottom edge of sweater, turn.

Rep Rows 2–7 across bottom edge of sweater, adjust as needed to end with Row 4 of patt. Do not fasten off.

Second Gusset

Row 1: Ch 1, 3 hdc in first st, hdc in next 4 sts, 3 hdc in each row-end st across right side of Front to marker, turn.

Rep Rows 2–14 (14, 14, 14, 14, 20) of First Gusset.

Back Bottom Edging

Rep Front Bottom Edging, joining to Back bottom edge. Fasten off, leaving a long tail for sewing. Working through blp, sew last row of edging to foundation ch at base of first row of first gusset.

→ **Note:** *Edging is worked around entire circumference of lower edge and side gussets are complete, but one gusset is joined to the back and the other is joined to the front. The completion of seams will be worked simultaneously with armhole opening trim.*

Assembly Diagram

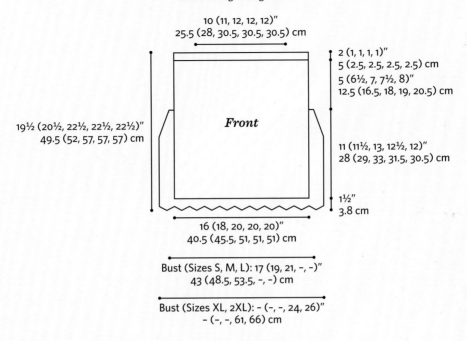

10 (11, 12, 12, 12)"
25.5 (28, 30.5, 30.5, 30.5) cm

2 (1, 1, 1, 1)"
5 (2.5, 2.5, 2.5, 2.5) cm
5 (6½, 7, 7½, 8)"
12.5 (16.5, 18, 19, 20.5) cm

Front

19½ (20½, 22½, 22½, 22½)"
49.5 (52, 57, 57, 57) cm

11 (11½, 13, 12½, 12)"
28 (29, 33, 31.5, 30.5) cm

1½"
3.8 cm

16 (18, 20, 20, 20)"
40.5 (45.5, 51, 51, 51) cm

Bust (Sizes S, M, L): 17 (19, 21, –, –)"
43 (48.5, 53.5, –, –) cm

Bust (Sizes XL, 2XL): – (–, –, 24, 26)"
– (–, –, 61, 66) cm

Assembly

Refer to assembly diagram.

With RS tog, sew Front to Back across shoulders, leaving center 10 (11, 12, 12, 12)" open for neck.

Joining Row

Row 1: With RS of First Gussett and left Front edge tog, pin top of Gusset to left Front at marker, join yarn with sl st at bottom of gussett, working through double thickness, loosely sl st in each st of gusset and evenly spaced across row-end sts of front to marker. Do not fasten off.

Armhole Trim

→ **Note:** *Work now progresses in rnds.*

Rnd 1: Turn sweater right side out; with RS facing, ch 1, sc evenly around armhole opening, sl st in first sc at beg of rnd to join.

Rnd 2: Ch 1, *sc in next 3 sts, ch-3 picot; rep from * around, sl st in first sc to join. Fasten off.

Rep Joining Row and Armhole Trim on other side of sweater.

Weave in loose ends. Block as desired.

Palmira SHAWL

This top-down shawl begins with the simplest of stitches and increases: double crochet with increases on each edge and double increases in the middle of every row. I chose a variety of edgings to manipulate into lace panels, working them differently to wrap the middle point of the shawl. I think it would make a stunning wedding shawl.

MATERIALS

Yarn: Valley Yarns Alpaca/Silk (80% alpaca/20% silk; 1,736 yd [1,587 m] per cone); Periwinkle, one ½ lb (227 g) cone.

Hook: E/4 (3.5 mm) or size needed to obtain gauge.

Notions: Stitch marker.

GAUGE

18 sts and 10 rows = 4" (10 cm) in dc after blocking.

FINISHED SIZE

62" wide × 30" long (157.5 × 76 cm).
Note: For a smaller shawlette, simply end the shawl at the desired size.

Shawl

First Solid Section

Refer to Stitch Diagram A.

Row 1: Ch 3 (counts as dc), 6 dc in 3rd ch from hook—7 dc.

Row 2: Ch 3 (counts as dc here and throughout), dc in first st (inc made), dc in each of next 2 sts, 3 dc in next st, dc in each of next 2 sts, 2 dc in last st— 11 dc.

Row 3: Ch 3, dc in first st, dc in each of next 4 sts, 3 dc in next st, dc in each of next 4 sts, 2 dc in last st—15 sts. Place marker in center st and move marker up as work progresses.

Row 4: Ch 3, dc in first st, dc in each st across to center st, 3 dc in center st, dc in each st across to last st, 2 dc in last st—19 dc.

Rows 5–12: Rep Row 4—51 dc at end of last row. Do not fasten off.

First Edging Insertion Panel

Refer to Stitch Diagram B.

→ **Note:** *Panel is worked in rows that are perpendicular to Row 12 of the prev section, joining to that row with a sl st at the end of every odd-numbered row.*

Row 1: Ch 17, 4 dc in 12th ch from hook, ch 5, sk first 3 sts on Row 12 of shawl, sl st in next st, ch 5, turn.

Row 2: Dc in next 4 dc, ch 11, turn.

Row 3: Dc in next 4 dc, ch 5, sk next 3 sts on Row 12, sl st in next st, ch 5, turn.

Rows 4–11: Rep Rows 2–3 four times.

Row 12: Rep Row 2.

Row 13: Dc in next 4 dc, ch 5, sk next st on Row 12, sl st in next marked st, ch 5, turn.

Row 14: Rep Row 2.

Row 15: Dc in next 4 sts, ch 5, sl st in same marked st on Row 12, ch 5, turn.

Row 16: Rep Row 2.

Row 17: Rep Row 15.

Row 18: Rep Row 2.

Row 19: Rep Row 13.

Stitch Diagram A

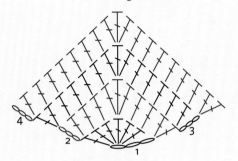

First Solid Section

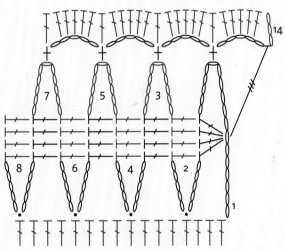

First Edging Insertion Panel

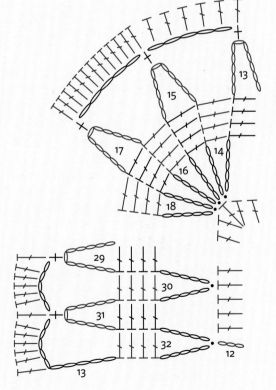

Stitch Diagram B

Row 20: Rep Row 2.

Row 21: Rep Row 3.

Rows 22–31: Rep Rows 2–3 five times.

Row 32: Dc in next 4 dc. Do not fasten off.

Second Solid Section

→ **Note:** *Row numbers cont from first solid section. Second solid section is worked in horizontal rows across side edge of first edging panel.*

Row 13: Ch 10 (counts as dtr, ch 5), sc in next ch-11 sp, *ch 5, sc in next ch-11 sp; rep from * across, ch 5, dtr in ch at base of 4 dc from Row 1 of insertion panel—17 ch-5 sps.

Row 14: Ch 3, [5 dc in next ch-5 sp, dc in next sc] 8 times, 11 dc in next ch-5 sp, [dc in next sc, 5 dc in next ch-5 sp, dc in next sc] 8 times, dc in 5th ch of beg ch-10, turn—109 dc. Place marker in center st and move marker up as work progresses.

Row 15: Ch 3, dc in first st, dc in each st across to center st, 3 dc in center st, dc in each st across to last st, 2 dc in last st—113 dc.

Rows 16–26: Rep Row 15—157 dc at end of last row. Do not fasten off.

Second Edging Insertion Panel

→ **Note:** *This panel is based on side-to-side Flower-fringed Web edging (see page 64). Panel is worked in rows that are perpendicular to Row 26 of the prev section, joining to that row with a sl st at the end of every odd-numbered row.*

Row 1: Ch 13, dc in 4th ch from hook, ch 11, sk next 11 ch, 2 dc in last ch, sk next 2 sts on Row 26 of shawl, sl st in next st, turn.

Row 2: Sl st in sp between first 2 dc, ch 3, dc in same sp, ch 5, sc under next 2 ch-11 lps, ch 5, sk next dc, 2 dc in sp before last dc, turn.

Row 3: Ch 8, sl st in 6th ch from hook to form a ring, ch 2, sk next dc, 2 dc in sp before next dc, ch 11, sk next ch-11 sp, sk next dc, 2 dc in sp before last dc, sk next 2 sts on Row 26, sl st in next st, turn.

Row 4: Sl st in sp between first 2 dc, ch 3, dc in same sp, ch 11, sk next ch-11 lp, sk next dc, 2 dc in sp before last dc, (2-dc cl, [ch 2, 2-dc cl] 5 times) in next ch-6 ring, sk next row-end st, sl st in next row-end st, turn, (sl st, ch 3, 2-dc cl, ch 3, sl st) in next 5 ch-2 sps, turn.

Row 5: Sl st in sp between first 2 dc, ch 3, dc in same sp, ch 5, sc under next 2 ch-11 lps, ch 5, sk next dc, 2 dc in sp before last dc, sk next 2 sts on Row 26, sl st in next st, turn.

Row 6: Sl st in sp between 2 dc, ch 3, dc in same sp, ch 11, sk next ch-11 lp, sk next dc, 2 dc in sp before last dc, turn.

Row 7: Sl st in sp between first 2 dc, ch 3, dc in same sp, ch 11, sk next ch-11 lp, sk next dc, 2 dc in sp before last dc, sk next 2 sts on Row 26, sl st in next st, turn.

Row 8: Sl st in sp between first 2 dc, ch 3, dc in same sp, ch 5, sc under next 2 ch-11 lps, ch 5, sk next dc, 2 dc in sp before last dc, turn.

Rows 9–106: Rep Rows 3–8 six times; rep Rows 3–5 once; cont to work in patt for next 12 rows, skipping only 1 st on Row 26 between joinings, ending with Row 5 of pattern; then work in patt across to end of Row 26, ending with Row 5 of patt, turn. Do not fasten off.

Third Solid Section

→ **Note:** *Row numbers cont from second solid section. This solid section is worked in horizontal rows across side edge of second edging panel, folding scallops to front and working in row-end dc only.*

Row 27: Ch 3, 5 dc in first row-end dc, 3 dc in each of next 50 row-end sts, 5 dc in next row-end dc, 7 dc in next row-end dc, 5 dc in next row-end dc, 3 dc row-end dc across, turn—329 dc. Place marker in center st and move marker up as work progresses.

Row 28: Ch 3, dc in first st, dc in each st across to center st, 3 dc in center st, dc in each st across to last st, 2 dc in last st—333 dc.

Rows 29-38: Rep Row 28—377 dc at end of last row. Do not fasten off.

Third Edging Insertion Panel

→ **Note:** *This panel is based on top-down Closed Leaf edging (see page 27).*

Row 1: Ch 10, sc in 2nd ch from hook and in each of next 8 ch (leaf center made), sc in each of next 5 sts on Row 38 of shawl, *ch 10, sc in 2nd ch from hook and in each of next 8 ch**, sc in each of next 10 sts on Row 38*; rep from * to * 17 times, [ch 10, sc in 2nd ch from hook and in each of next 8 ch, sc in each of next 3 sts on Row 38] twice; rep from * to * 18 times, ch 10, sc in 2nd ch from hook and in each of next 8 ch, sc in each of next 5 sts on Row 38; rep from * to ** once, sc in last st, turn—41 leaf centers made.

Row 2: Ch 1, *over next 8 sts on prev row, sc in next 2 sc, hdc in next 2 sc, dc in next 2 sc, tr in next 2 sc, 4 tr in next sc, ch-4 picot, working in back side of chains, 4 tr in next ch, tr in next 2 ch, dc in next 2 ch, hdc in next 2 ch, sc in next 2 ch**, sc in each sc across to next leaf center; rep from * across, ending last rep at **, sc in last sc, turn—41 leaves made.

Row 3: Sl st in next 12 sts, sl st in next picot, ch 1, sc in same picot, *ch 7, sk 2 sts, yo twice, insert hook in next st, (yo, pull through 2 lps twice), sk 2 sts, yo 3 times, insert hook in next st, (yo, pull through 2 lps) 3 times, sk next 6 sts on this leaf, all sc between petals and next 6 sts on next leaf, yo 3 times, insert hook in next st, (yo, pull through 2 lps) 3 times, sk next 2 sts, yo twice, insert hook in next st, (yo, pull through 2 lps twice), yo, pull through all 5 lps on hook (2tr/2dtr cl worked), ch 7, sc in next ch-4 picot; rep from * across, turn. Do not fasten off.

Fourth Solid Section

→ **Note:** *Row numbers cont from third solid section. This section is worked in horizontal rows across top edge of third edging panel.*

Row 39: Ch 3, 7 dc first ch-7 sp, 5 dc in next 38 ch-7 sps, 9 dc in next ch-7 sp, 5 dc in next 38 ch-7 sps, 8 dc in last ch-7 sp, turn—415 dc. Place marker in center st and move marker up as work progresses.

Rows 40-44: Ch 3, 2 dc in first st, dc in each st across to center st, 3 dc in center st, dc in each st across to last st, 3 dc in last st—445 dc.

Rows 45-50: Ch 3, dc in first st, dc in each st across to center st, 3 dc in center st, dc in each st across to last st, 2 dc in last st—469 dc. Do not fasten off.

Fourth Edging Panel

→ **Note:** *Fourth edging panel is based on top-down Gothic Cathedral edging (see page 28).*

Row 1: Ch 1, sc in first 4 sts, ch 5, sk 4 sts, dc2tog over next 2 sts, *ch 5, sk 4 sts, sc in each of next 3 sts, turn, [ch 2, dc] 3 times in next ch-5 sp, ch 2, (dc, ch 5, dc) in next dc2tog, [ch 2, dc] 3 times in next ch-5 sp, sk next 2 sc, sl st in next sc, turn, [ch 2, dc in next dc] 4 times, ch 2, (dc, ch 5, dc) in next ch-5 sp, [ch 2, dc in next dc] 4 times, sc in each of next 5 sc in prev row, *ch 5, sk 4 sts, dc2tog over next 2 sts, ch 5, sk 4 sts, sc in each of next 3 sts, turn, [ch 2, dc] 3 times in next ch-5 sp, ch 2, (dc, ch 5, dc) in next dc2tog, [ch 2, dc] 3 times in next ch-5 sp, sk next 2 sc, sl st in next sc, turn, [ch 2, dc in next dc] 3 times, ch 9, turn, sk next 5 ch-2 sps, sl st in next dc, turn, ([3 sc, ch-3 picot] 3 times, 3 sc) in next ch-9 lp, sl st in next dc, ch 2, dc in next dc, ch 2, (dc, ch 5, dc) in next ch-5 sp, [ch 2, dc in next dc] 4 times**, sc in each of next 5 sc in prev row; rep from * across, ending last rep at **, sc in last 2 sc.

Fasten off and weave in loose ends. Block as desired.

Memphis BAG

The flower adorning this bag is crocheted right onto the bag without sewing. The bag itself is a simple design of square motifs and a deep-set gusset. The addition of strategically placed back-loop-only stitches allows for simple joining points for applying the flower as you go.

MATERIALS

Yarn: Patons Grace (100% mercerized cotton; 136 yd [125 m] per 50 g [1.75 oz]); #26440 Lotus blue (A), 5 skeins.

Patons Lace (80% acrylic/10% mohair/10% wool; 498 yd [455 m] per 85 g [3 oz]); #33550 Bonfire (B), 1 skein.

Hooks: E/4 (3.5 mm) and G/6 (4 mm) or sizes needed to obtain gauge.

Notions: One pair 12" (30.5 cm) leather purse handles.

GAUGE

First 3 rnds of front = 3" (7.6 cm) square; 22 sts = 4" (10 cm).

FINISHED SIZE

14" wide × 13" deep (35.5 × 33 cm) excluding handles.

Front

Refer to Stitch Diagram A.

With smaller hook and A, ch 5, sl st in 5th ch from hook to form ring.

Rnd 1 (RS): Ch 3 (counts as dc here and throughout), 2 dc in ring, (ch 3, 3 dc) 3 times in ring, ch 3, sl st in top of beg ch-3 to join—4 ch-3 sps.

Rnd 2: Ch 3, *dc-tbl in each st across to next ch-3 sp, dc-tbl in next ch, (dc-tbl, ch 3, dc-tbl) in next ch, dc-tbl in next ch; rep from * around, sl st in top of beg ch-3 to join.

Rnds 3–11: Ch 3, *dc-tbl in each st across to next ch-3 sp, dc-tbl in next ch, (dc-tbl, ch 3, dc-tbl) in next ch, dc-tbl in next ch; rep from * around, dc-tbl in each st across to beg, sl st in top of beg ch-3 to join.

Fasten off.

Gussets

→ **Note:** *With short-row shaping, the next rows will create the side gussets and bottom for each half of the bag.*

Row 1: With RS facing, join A in 31st dc to the left of any corner ch-3 sp, ch 1, *sc in each dc across to next corner, 3 sc in corner ch-3 sp; rep from * once, sc in each of next 33 dc, turn—135 sc.

Row 2: Ch 1, sc in each sc across, working in row below, sc in next 5 dc, turn—140 sc.

Rows 3–13: Rep Row 2—195 sc at end of last row. Fasten off.

Back

Work as for Front, but do not fasten off.

Seaming front to back

With WS of Front and Back tog, and RS of Front facing, working through double thickness, matching sts, sl st in each st across side, bottom and next side. Do not fasten off.

Cuff

→ **Note:** *Work in rnds at the top opening of purse. This will be folded over to the inside at the end.*

Rnd 1: Ch 1, sc in each st around top edge of Front and Back, sl st in first sc to join—132 sts.

Rnds 2–6: Ch 1, sc in each st around, sl st in first sc to join. Fasten off.

Flower

Refer to Stitch Diagram B.

→ **Note:** *The 3-dimensional flower begins with a rnd of 2 dc in each free lp of Rnds 1–11, beg at the center, spiraling out from each rnd with a ch-3 to travel to the next exterior rnd of free lps.*

With larger hook, join B with sl st in free lp of any st in Rnd 1 of front of purse.

Stitch Diagram A

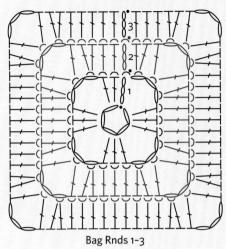

Bag Rnds 1–3

Stitch Diagram B

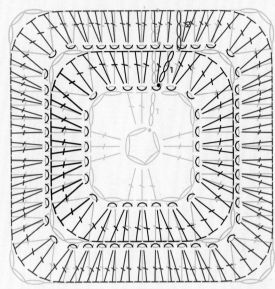

Flower Rnds 1–2

Stitch Diagram C

Repeat

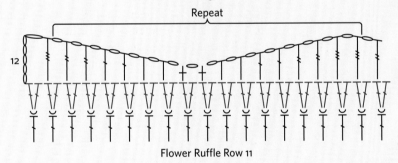

Flower Ruffle Row 11

Rnd 1: Ch 3, dc in same st, work 2 dc in free lp of each st around. Do not join.

Rnd 2: Ch 3 to get to Rnd 2 of Front, 2 dc in free lp of each st in Rnd 2.

Rnds 3–10: Ch 3 to get to next rnd of Front, 2 dc in free lp of each st around. At end of Rnd 10, turn.

Refer to Stitch Diagram C.

Row 11: Ch 6 (counts as dtr, ch 1), working across sts made in last 8 continuous rnds, sk next st, dtr

in next st, *(ch 1, sk 1 st, tr in next st) twice, (ch 1, sk 1 st, dc in next st) twice, (ch 1, sk 1 st, hdc in next st) twice, (ch 1, sk 1 st, sc in next st) twice, (ch 1, sk 1 st, hdc in next st) twice, (ch 1, sk 1 st, dc in next st) twice, (ch 1, sk 1 st, tr in next st) twice, (ch 1, sk 1 st, dtr in next st) twice; rep from * around until you have spiraled back to the center of the flower, but stop at Rnd 3 (you will have 2 small center spirals unworked from Rnds 1 and 2 of flower (see photo). Fasten off and weave in loose ends.

Petra WRAP SKIRT

This skirt is worked sideways, which makes for an incredibly easy pattern to modify for additional sizes. The pleats add textural interest, and the tiered edging adds a great splash of color with a deceptively simple technique.

MATERIALS

Yarn: Naturally Caron Spa (75% microdenier acrylic/25% rayon from bamboo; 251 yd [230 m] per 3 oz [85 g]); #0002 Coral Lipstick (A), 4 skeins (see Notes); #0014 Rosalinda (B), 1 skein.

Hook: H/8 (5 mm) or size needed to obtain gauge.

Notions: Removable stitch marker.

GAUGE

16 sts = 4" (10 cm); 6 rows in skirt pattern = 3" (7.6 cm).

FINISHED SIZE

Sizing (circumference at low waist) is customizable. Sample shown is 36" (91.5 cm) in circumference before joining tie; bottom edge is 90" (229 cm) in circumference; length is 19" (48 cm).

Notes

❋ Skirt pattern is based on side-to-side Lace Column Scallops Edging II; see stitch dictionary for diagram (page 60).

❋ Skirt is worked from side to side, then the top edge is gathered into pleats to form the waistband. To customize fit, repeat Rows 2–7 until work is 3 times desired waistband circumference. You may need more or less yarn than indicated; please plan accordingly.

Skirt

With A, ch 70.

Row 1 (RS): Sc in 2nd ch from hook and each ch across, turn—69 sc.

Row 2: Ch 4, tr in same st (counts as 2-tr cl), *ch 1, sk 1 st, 2-tr cl in next st; rep from * across, turn.

Row 3: Ch 1, sc in same st, *sc in next ch-1 sp, sc in next st; rep from * across, turn.

Row 4: Ch 3 (counts as dc here and throughout), sk first st, dc in each of next 2 sts, *ch 3, sk 3 sts, dc in each of next 3 sts; rep from * across, turn.

Row 5: Ch 6 (counts as dc, ch 3 here and throughout), sk first 3 sts, 3 dc in next ch-3 sp, *ch 3, sk 3 dc, 3 dc in next ch-3 sp; rep from * across, ending with ch 3, sk 2 sts, dc in top of ch-3, turn.

Row 6: Ch 3, 2 dc in ch-3 sp, *ch 3, sk 3 sts, 3 dc in next ch-3 sp; rep from * across, (ch 2, tr) 6 times in

next row-end st, sk next row, sl st in end of next sc row, turn, [sl st, ch 3, 2-dc cl, ch 3, sl st] in next 6 ch-2 sps.

Row 7: *Sc in next 3 dc**, 3 sc in next ch-3 sp; rep from * across, ending last rep at **, turn.

Rep Rows 2–7 for pattern, ending with Row 7.

Rep Rows 2–7 twenty-nine times or to desired width (see Notes).

Second tier of edging

With RS facing, join B with sl st in side of last tr at end of Row 2 on scallop side of edging.

Row 1: Ch 6 (counts as tr, ch 2), work [(tr, ch 2) 5 times, tr] in same row-end st, working behind scallops, sk next 2 row-end sts, sl st in next row-end st at base of prev scallop, turn, 2 sc in next 6 ch-2 sps, turn, [sl st in next st, ch 3, dc2tog over next same st and next st, ch 3, sl st in same st] 6 times, *sk next 2 row-end sts, [(tr, ch 2) 6 times, tr] in next row-end tr, working behind scallops, sk next

2 row-end sts, sl st in next row-end st at base of prev scallop, turn, 2 sc in next 6 ch-2 sps, turn, [sl st in next st, ch 3, dc2tog over next same st and next st, ch 3, sl st in same st] 6 times; rep from * across.

Pleating row and waistband

Working along ends of rows to create pleats, crochet through 3 thicknesses as foll:

Row 1: With RS facing, join B with sl st in top-right corner on waist edge of skirt, ch 1, sc in side edge of sc, *insert hook from front to back in next row-end tr, insert hook from back to front in next row-end dc, sk next row-end dc, insert hook from front to back in next row-end dc (3 thicknesses on hook), work 4 sc in same sp of 3 layers; rep from * across, 4 sc in next row-end tr, sc in last row-end sc, turn—122 sc.

Rows 2–6: Ch 1, sc in each st across, turn. Do not fasten off.

Ties

Working along side edge of the 6 rows of waistband:

Row 1: Ch 3 (counts as dc), dc in each of next 5 row-end sts, turn—6 dc.

Row 2: Sk 3 sts, sl st in sp before next st, ch 3 (counts as dc), 5 dc in same sp, turn.

Rows 3–48: Rep Row 2. Fasten off.

Try on skirt and mark where the fronts overlap and place marker. This is the position for joining the second tie.

Row 1: With RS facing, join B with sl st around the post of sc in Row 1 at marker, ch 3 (counts as dc), working across depth of waistband, dc around the post of next 5 sc, turn—6 dc.

Row 2: Sk 3 sts, sl st in sp before next st, ch 3 (counts as dc), 5 dc in same sp, turn.

Rows 3–48: Rep Row 2. Fasten off. Weave in loose ends.

Babylonia HAT

This hat is worked from the top down in a spiral of Bruges lace that increases in length as you join the next strip to the previous one using long chains. While Bruges lace is two-dimensional, I find the staggered geometric patterning is reminiscent of the three-dimensional, lush Babylonian gardens.

MATERIALS

Yarn: Filatura Di Crosa Zarina (100% merino superwash; 181 yd [165 m] per 50 g [1.75 oz]); 1527 light green, 1 ball.

Hook: D/3 (3.25 mm) or size needed to obtain gauge.

GAUGE

First 17 rows = 3" (7.5 cm) in diameter; 10 rows in shell patt = 4" (10 cm).

FINISHED SIZE

20" (51 cm) circumference at top edge of brim.

Notes

❋ See diagram with Graduated Shells in Bruges Lace on page 49.

❋ Rows of shells are worked around and joined to the center point at the top of the hat to form the first section. Shells are worked around preceding section in a spiral until depth of hat measures 7″ (18 cm). Then rows of hdc are worked around in vertical rows and joined to bottom edging to form the brim.

Note: *First section of spiral complete—you should have 8 ch-7 lps around perimeter of work.*

Row 17: Rep Row 1.

Row 18: Ch 3, sl st in next ch-7 sp in preceding section, ch 3, sk 2 dc, 4 dc in sp before next st, turn.

Row 19: Rep Row 1.

Row 20: Ch 3, sl st in same ch-7 sp in Row 1, ch 3, sk 2 dc, 4 dc in sp before next st, turn.

Rows 21–48: Rep Rows 17–20 seven times.

Row 49: Rep Row 1.

Row 50: Ch 3, sl st in next ch-7 sp in preceding section, ch 3, sk 2 dc, 4 dc in sp before next st, turn.

Rows 51–54: Rep Rows 17–20 once.

Rows 55–98: Rep Rows 49–54 eight times.

Row 99: Rep Row 1.

Row 100: Rep Row 50.

Rep Rows 99–100 until hat measures 7" deep from beg, ending with an even-numbered row (a joining row) of pattern.

Next row: Ch 7, sk 2 dc, 4 dc in sp before next st, ch 3, sl st in adjacent ch-7 sp. Do not fasten off.

Hat

Refer to Stitch Diagram A.

Set-up row (RS): Ch 8 (counts as ch-7 lp and 1 ch for working sts), 4 dc in 8th ch from hook, turn.

Row 1: Ch 7, sk 2 dc, 4 dc in sp before next st, turn.

Row 2: Ch 3, sl st in ch-7 sp at beg of set-up row, ch 3, sk 2 dc, 4 dc in sp before next st, turn.

Row 3: Rep Row 1.

Row 4: Ch 3, sl st in ch-7 sp in set-up row, ch 3, sk 2 dc, 4 dc in sp before next st, turn.

Rows 5–16: Rep Rows 3–4 six more times.

Brim

Refer to Stitch Diagram B.

Row 1: Ch 2 (counts as hdc), 3 hdc in next ch-3 sp, hdc-tbl in each of next 4 sts, 3 hdc in next ch-7 sp, turn—11 sts.

Row 2: Ch 2 (counts as hdc), hdc-tbl in each st across, sl st in same ch-7 sp as prev row.

Row 3: Turn, sk sl st, hdc-tbl in each st across—11 sts.

Row 4: Ch 2 (counts as hdc), hdc-tbl in each st across, sl st in next ch-7 sp.

Row 5: Rep Row 3.

Stitch Diagram A

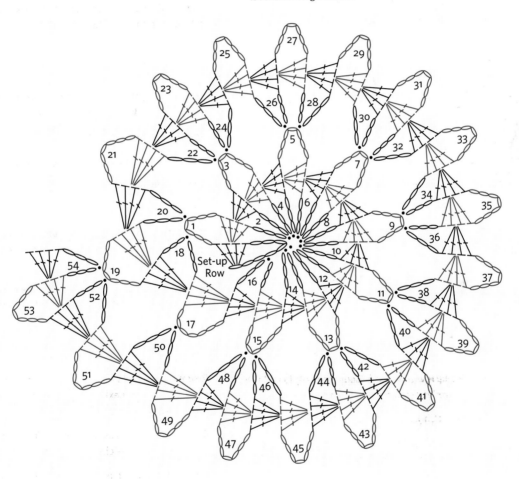

Stitch Diagram B

Brim

12

10

8

7

6

5

4

3

2

1

Next
Row

224

223

Stitch Diagram C

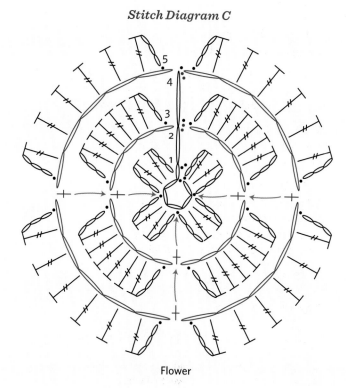

5

4

3

2

1

Flower

Row 6: Ch 2 (counts as hdc), hdc-tbl in each st across, sl st in same ch-7 sp as prev row.

Rows 7–98: Rep Rows 3–6 until brim is joined to each ch-7 sp around.

Next 8 rows: Ch 2, hdc-tbl in each st across, turn. Do not fasten off.

Flower

Refer to Stitch Diagram C.

Rnd 1: Ch 8, sl st in 5th ch from hook to form ring, sl st in next ch (counts as sc), work (ch 3, 4 tr, ch 3, sl st) 4 times in ring, sl st in first sl st to join.

Rnd 2: Sl st in next ch (counts as sc), *ch 5, working behind petals of Rnd 1, sc in next sl st; rep from * 3 more times, omitting last sc, sl st in next ch to join.

Rnd 3: *(Sl st, ch 3, 6 tr, ch 3, sl st) in next ch-5 sp; rep from * 3 more times, sl st in first sl st at beg of rnd to join.

Rnd 4: Sl st in next ch (counts as sc), *ch 5, working behind petals of Rnd 3, sc in next ch-5 ring between 3rd and 4th sts from prev rnd (see illustration), ch 5, sc in next sl st; rep from * 3 more times, omitting last sc, sl st in first sl st to join.

Rnd 5: *(Sl st, ch 3, 6 tr, ch 3, sl st) in next ch-5 sp; rep from * 5 more times, sl st in first sl st to join. Fasten off, leaving long tail.

Finishing

Using long tail, sew overlap flap of brim to attached side of brim. Sew petals of flower to double thickness of brim of hat to secure.

Wash, block to finished measurements, and let dry. Weave in loose ends.

Resources

Bijou Basin Ranch
PO Box 154
Elbert, CO 80106
bijoubasinranch.com
Llasa Wilderness

Tahki-Stacy Charles Inc.
70-30 83rd St., Bldg. #12
Glendale, NY 11385
tahkistacycharles.com
Filatura di Crosa Zarina; Filatura di Crosa Superior

Malabrigo Yarn
malabrigoyarn.com
Lace

Bernat Yarn
Distributed by Spinrite LP
320 Livingstone Ave. S.
Box 40
Listowel, ON
Canada N4W 3H3
bernat.com
Mosaic

Caron International
Distributed by Spinrite LP
320 Livingstone Ave. S.
Box 40
Listowel, ON
Canada N4W 3H3
caron.com
Stitch.Rock.Love Sheep(ish); Naturally Caron Country; Naturally Caron Spa

Patons
Distributed by Spinrite LP
320 Livingstone Ave. S.
Box 40
Listowel, ON
Canada N4W 3H3
patonsyarns.com
Grace; Lace

WEBS—America's Yarn Store
75 Service Center Rd.
Northampton, MA 01060
yarn.com
Valley Yarn's Alpaca 2/14

Glossary

blp	back loop (only)
ch(s)	chain(s)
cont	continue/continuing
dc	double crochet
foll	follows/following
flp	front loop (only)
hdc	half double crochet
lp(s)	loop(s)

prev	previous
rep	repeat
rnd(s)	round(s)
sc	single crochet
sl st	slip stitch
st(s)	stitch(es)
tbl	through the back loop (only)
tr	treble (triple) crochet

Spike treble crochet (*spike tr*)

Yo twice, insert hook in st 2 rows below, pull up a lp elongating yarn until you are at the top of the last row worked, (yo, pull through 2 lps) 3 times.

Spike treble crochet 3 together (*spike tr3tog*)

*Yo twice, insert hook in specified st 2 rows below, pull up a lp elongating yarn until you are at the top of the last row worked, (yo, pull through 2 lps) twice; rep from * 2 more times, yo, pull through all 4 lps on hook.

Double treble crochet (*dtr*)

Yo 3 times, insert hook in specified st and pull up a lp, (yo, pull through 2 lps) 4 times.

Triple treble crochet (*trtr*)

Yo 4 times, insert hook in specified st and pull up a lp, (yo, pull through 2 lps) 5 times.

Front post single crochet (*fpsc*)

Insert hook from front to back around the post of the indicated stitch on previous row and pull up a lp, pull through 2 lps on hook.

Extended treble crochet (*etr*)

Yo twice, insert hook in specified st, yo and pull up a lp (4 lps on hook), yo, pull through 1 lp, (yo, pull through 2 lps on hook) 3 times.

Extended double treble crochet (*edtr*)

Yo 3 times, insert hook in specified st, yo and pull up a lp (5 lps on hook), yo, pull through 1 lp, (yo, pull through 2 lps on hook) 4 times.

Reverse single crochet (*reverse sc*)

Working from right to left, insert hook in specified st and pull up a lp, yo, pull through 2 lps on hook.

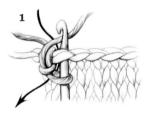

1

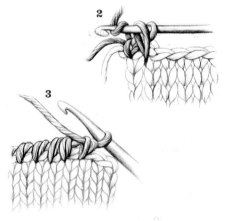

2

3

Ch-3 picot

Ch 3, sl st in 3rd ch from hook.

Ch-4 picot

Ch 4, sl st in 4th ch from hook.

3-tr cluster (*3-tr cl*)

*Yo twice, insert hook in specified st and pull up a lp, (yo, pull through 2 lps) 2 times; rep from * 2 more times (4 lps on hook), yo, pull through all 4 lps on hook.

2-tr/2-dtr cluster

Yo 3 times, insert hook in next st, [yo, pull through 2 lps] 3 times, sk next 2 sts, yo twice, insert hook in next st, (yo, pull through 2 lps) twice, yo, pull through all 5 lps on hook.

3-dtr cluster

*Yo 3 times, insert hook in specified st and pull up a lp, [yo, pull through 2 lps] 3 times; rep from * 2 more times (4 lps on hook), yo, pull through all 4 lps on hook.

Foundation single crochet (*fsc*)

Start with a slipknot on hook, ch 2, insert hook in 2nd ch from hook and draw up a lp, yo, draw through 1 lp, yo, and draw through 2 lps—1 single crochet with its own chain at bottom. Work next st under lps of that chain. Insert hook under 2 lps at bottom of the previous st, draw up a lp, yo and draw through 1 lp, yo and draw through 2 lps. Repeat for length of foundation.

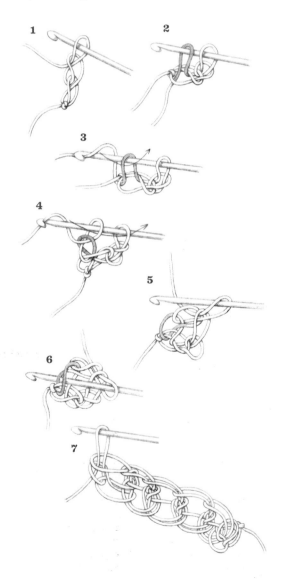

Hdc3tog

[Yo, insert hook in next st and pull up a lp] 3 times, yo and pull through all lps on hook.

Dc2tog

*Yo, insert hook in next st and pull up a lp, yo and pull through 2 lps on hook; rep from * once more, yo and pull through all 3 lps on hook.

Dc3tog

*Yo, insert hook in next st and pull up a lp, yo and pull through 2 lps on hook; rep from * twice more, yo and pull through all 4 lps on hook.

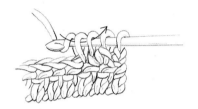

2-dc cluster

Yo, insert hook in next st and pull up a lp, yo and pull through 2 lps on hook, insert hook in same st and pull up a lp, yo and pull through 2 lps on hook, yo and pull through all 3 lps on hook.

3-dc cluster

Yo, insert hook in next st and pull up a lp, yo and pull through 2 lps on hook, [insert hook in same st and pull up a lp, yo and pull through 2 lps on hook] twice, yo and pull through all 4 lps on hook.

Tr2tog

*Yo twice, insert hook in next st and pull up a lp, [yo and pull through 2 lps on hook] twice; rep from * once more, yo and pull through all lps on hook.

Index

Longing for more inspiration from Kristin?

Look no further.

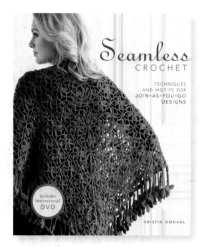

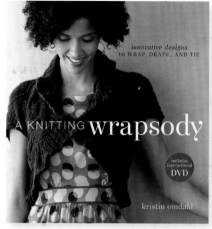

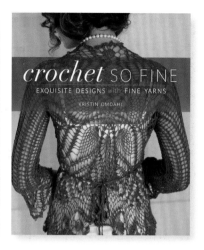

Seamless Crochet + DVD
Techniques and Designs for
Join-As-You-Go Motifs
Kristin Omdahl
ISBN 978-1-59668-297-9
$24.95

**A Knitting Wrapsody
+ DVD**
Innovative Designs
to Wrap, Drape, and Tie
Kristin Omdahl
ISBN 978-1-59668-307-5
$24.95

Crochet So Fine
Exquisite Designs
with Fine Yarns
Kristin Omdahl
ISBN 978-1-59668-198-9
$22.95

crochet*me* shop
shop.crochetme.com

INTERWEAVE CROCHET

From cover to cover, *Interweave Crochet* magazine
presents great projects for the beginner to the
advanced crocheter. Every issue is packed full of
captivating designs, step-by-step instructions, easy-
to-understand illustrations, plus well-written, lively
articles sure to inspire. **Interweavecrochet.com**

fueling the crochet revolution

Want to CrochetMe? *Crochet Me* is an online
community that shares your passion for all things
crochet. Browse through our free patterns, read our
blogs, check out our galleries, chat in the forums,
make a few friends. Sign up at **Crochetme.com**.